200 MORE

Brief, Creative & Practical

Art Therapy
Techniques

A Guide for Clinicians & Clients

Susan I. Buchalter, ATR-BC, CGP, LPC

Published by
PESI Publishing & Media
PESI, Inc
3839 White Ave
Eau Claire, WI 54703

Cover: Amy Rubenzer
Editing: Jenessa Jackson, PhD
Layout: Amy Rubenzer & Bookmasters

ISBN: 9781683732693

Printed in the United States of America.

PESI
Publishing
& Media
pesipublishing.com

acknowledgement

Thank you to Dr. Alan H. Katz for his superb technical support.

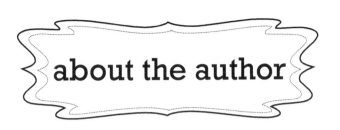

about the author

Susan I. Buchalter, ATR-BC, CGP, LPC, is a senior clinical therapist and art therapist at Penn Medicine - Princeton House Behavioral Health, where she introduced art therapy to doctors and staff members in the 1980s. She is a board-certified art therapist, licensed professional counselor, and certified group psychotherapist, and has spent over 30 years leading art therapy and psychotherapy groups. She is co-creator of the Garden State Art Therapy Association, now known as The New Jersey Art Therapy Association. She was an adjunct professor at Trenton State College (The College of New Jersey).

Susan is the author of *A Practical Art Therapy*; *Art Therapy Techniques and Applications*; *Art Therapy and Creative Coping Techniques for Older Adults*; *Mandala Symbolism and Techniques: Innovative Approaches for Professionals*; *Raising Self-Esteem in Adults: An Eclectic Approach with Art Therapy CBT and DBT-Based Techniques*; *250 Brief, Creative & Practical Art Therapy Techniques: A Guide for Clinicians & Clients*; *Stick Figure Affirmations: Cartoons to Lift the Spirit*; and *Mandaloodles: A Mini Doodle-Filled Mandala Coloring Book*. She maintains a private practice in Lawrenceville, New Jersey.

table of contents

introduction

This focus of this book is to empower clients through artistic means. In particular, it is intended to allow clients to communicate their thoughts, feelings, concerns, problems, hopes, dreams, and desires in a relatively non-threatening manner. As an expressive therapy, the arts provide clients a safe vehicle from which to express their unconscious, as well as conscious, issues and beliefs. It provides them the freedom to "draw from within" and express their inner and outer worlds in any way they choose. They can decide whether they want to use stick figures, lines, colors, shapes, abstractions, or realism to portray their thoughts. They can decide whether they want to use markers, oil pastels, or crayons as a medium, as well as what size drawing paper they would like to use. These choices are theirs, and there are no judgments. When clients are given the ability to make decisions such as these, it enhances their problem-solving skills and increases their independence and self-esteem.

In addition, art promotes self-awareness and healing as clients gain a better perspective of their problems and concerns. As clients work to create meaningful images and symbols, they are able to expend energy in a healthy manner, and they can experience a catharsis or release as they become focused and involved in the artwork. Moreover, creative expression provides clients an opportunity to document their thoughts and refer back to them as needed. In this way, they have the opportunity to view patterns of growth and change. They also experience a sense of accomplishment as they work to complete a project from start to finish. They are able to discover strengths they never knew they had, which they can relish for years to come.

By using the art therapy directives included in this book, you will provide a therapeutic platform from which clients can:

- Express and share their inner experiences in a visual way
- Have a healthy, creative outlet for intense feelings
- Learn creative stress management techniques
- Share their problems and concerns through artistic expression
- Experiment with and learn how to use a variety of media
- Develop self-awareness and identify areas of concern
- Develop talents and acknowledge their strengths, some of which have been long forgotten
- Be valued as part of a community that fosters non-judgment and acceptance

WHAT'S IN THIS BOOK

This book introduces a variety of predominantly brief, creative warm-up exercises that are intended to facilitate communication, connection, and creative expression among a wide variety of clients, as well as any individuals who want to gain greater creativity, introspection, and self-awareness. **Warm-ups are abridged techniques that generally take 5-10 minutes to complete. These techniques pave the way for clients to become involved and focused on longer, more introspective art therapy**

and psychotherapy groups. The goal is for clients to use these exercises as a form of "mental stretching" to help them learn how to think in the abstract and become comfortable with self-expression and self-exploration. As clients come to realize that there is no "right" or "wrong" way to approach the exercises, they soon learn that the **focus is on the process and not the final product.**

Similar to my previous publication, *250 Brief, Creative & Practical Art Therapy Techniques: A Guide for Clinicians & Clients,* each of the exercises in this book contain a description of the art therapy procedure, questions for exploration, and sample client responses. However, this book also contains an additional "benefits" section for each directive, which describes ways in which each specific exercise inspires and helps clients. This addition will allow you to share the practical goals of each technique in a way that is clear, simple and understandable for clients. Furthermore, although all of the exercises in this book have general benefits, some of them promote additional desired behaviors, actions, and activity. For example, if a client is withdrawn, a project that elicits more sharing and active participation, like collage work and interactive mandala design, might be preferable to a sketching exercise.

Each art therapy directive is explained in an easy and clear manner, and accompanying photos of clients' artwork are occasionally included throughout. This artwork has either been copied and re-drawn with clients' permission or designed to serve as an example solely for this publication. A few projects within this book are similar to one another, but different enough to justify including both in this publication because they are useful in working with clients. These exercises are indicated using Roman numerals for clarification.

While the focus of this book is on brief warm-up exercises, I have also included some exercises that take a little longer than most warm-ups, but can be modified if needed to suit specific time constraints and the needs and goals of the therapy group. The mask projects in particular may take two sessions to complete. However, I have found that clients enjoy and benefit significantly from the mask directives, which almost always prove insightful. Designing masks provides clients with the opportunity to express thoughts and feelings, fears, fantasies, personality characteristics, and core beliefs in a safe, relaxed manner.

WHO THIS BOOK IS FOR

This book is intended for art therapists, counselors, social workers, psychologists, teachers, and anyone interested in expanding their self-awareness and understanding of the way they view themselves and their environment.

HOW TO USE THIS BOOK

Many of the exercises in this book may be used for both individuals and groups; it is up to each therapist to decide which exercises are most therapeutic in a particular setting. In addition, therapists will need to decide which exercises are appropriate for their specific clients. For example, mindfulness may be therapeutic for a recovering addict, but not for a client diagnosed with schizophrenia. It is not uncommon for individuals with schizophrenia to have a difficult time sitting still, being introspective, and following guided imagery for more than a few minutes. Mindfulness exercises might make them anxious, especially if they hallucinate or have high anxiety.

To make it easier for therapists, teachers, psychologists, counselors, and individuals interested in continued self-exploration, the exercises in this book are categorized according to general themes. This will help you decide which exercises are most beneficial for the specific clients and types of groups you are leading. For example, the happiness exercises are most effective if the goal is to enhance mood and increase activity levels, whereas the self-awareness exercises are most appropriate if the goal is to increase clients' understanding of their own drives, personalities, habits, and values.

If you are using these exercises in a group setting, it is important to take the time to discuss each client's artwork, as each work of art serves as a compilation of the feelings, problems, concerns, and solutions that are exclusively the client's own. By allowing each group member to observe, analyze, and relate to the representations and figures that the other clients have created, you provide a forum from which they can interact with one another and get feedback. It provides group members an opportunity to reflect on the symbols that they (and others) have drawn, and to convey any thoughts that would otherwise not be shared verbally.

One final thought before you begin: As I have stated in my previous publications, this is not a cookbook of techniques but an array of ideas to help you pinpoint specific client needs and enhance the quality of the therapy group. My objective is to help individuals find ways to increase self-awareness and self-worth, better cope with problems, and ultimately increase their life satisfaction.

MATERIALS FOR WARM-UPS

You will need drawing paper, markers, oil pastels, crayons, gel pens, and/or colored pencils for most exercises. Clients appear to greatly enjoy using gel pens in particular, especially for detailed work. They derive pleasure from viewing the bright, dazzling colors, and the flow of the ink from the pen. If supplementary supplies (e.g., clay, paint, sequins) are optional for a particular exercise, then it is the discretion of the group leader whether or not to use them. Additional items that are pertinent to each project are noted.

TERMS USED

Mandala: Translated from Sanskrit to mean "circle," mandalas are used in art therapy to help clients express their feelings, find wholeness and clarity, heal and reduce stress, and practice mindfulness.

Collagette: Collagette is a mini-collage that is generally 4 × 6 or 5 × 7 inches in size. This technique is ideal if you just want a brief art therapy project or if you are working with clients who have short attention spans.

Sketch Collage: Coined by a client during an art therapy group, a sketch collage is a compilation of sketches or drawings that are organized on a piece of paper in a manner similar to that involved in creating a traditional collage.

chapter one
self-compassion

Self-compassion, as defined by Kristin Neff, has three aspects: kindness, common humanity, and mindfulness.[1] At its core, self-compassion entails being kind toward yourself and treating yourself the same way you would treat a good friend in a similar situation. It involves fully accepting who you are without judgment, regardless of any problems, failures, or perceived shortcomings you may have.

In essence, the focus of self-compassion is on giving yourself a break. We are all human, and everyone is just trying to get by the best they can. When we berate or criticize ourselves, this only leads to depression and stagnation; it doesn't motivate us to do better. In contrast, when we practice self-compassion, we give ourselves permission to receive mental hugs, take healthy risks, and accept that – sometimes – we will make mistakes and fail. It encourages us to forgive ourselves, learn from our errors, and move on with our lives. In turn, we are more likely to be motivated to push ourselves to work harder and have higher standards. For example, we are more likely to take healthy risks, such as applying for a new job, trying a new sport or hobby, or befriending someone who we may think is out of our league. We don't remain victims of our circumstances, and we don't allow others to control us because we feel worthy of respect and validation.

In addition, practicing self-compassion can enhance the quality of our relationships, as everyone benefits when we accept ourselves and don't judge our experiences, choices, abilities, or personality characteristics. Our disposition is often brighter, which enables us to become more loving, devoted friends and partners, as well as positive role models. Our family members, acquaintances, and co-workers can also notice the benefits when we treat ourselves in this kind, respectful, and "self-friendly" manner.[2]

The following self-compassion exercises are intended to help individuals become more self-aware and introspective. These exercises allow clients to examine healthy and unhealthy patterns of thinking, with the aim of increasing positive thinking and lessening or eliminating negative thinking and self-defeating behavior.

What's Inside My Heart

PROCEDURE: Create a symbol of your heart using whatever materials you like. Think about its size, shape, texture, and color. Add what is inside your heart, such as love, family and friends, admiration for yourself and others, or respect for humanity.

BENEFITS: This exercise helps you become aware of your strengths, positive qualities, and gifts that you have to give to yourself and others. In doing so, this exercise helps foster increased gratitude for all that you have to offer.

QUESTIONS FOR EXPLORATION:

1. What does your heart look like (e.g., how large is it)?

2. Is your heart currently strong or weak? Is it in one piece or broken?

3. How can you fill your heart with love and support?

4. What do you do that is heart-healthy, emotionally as well as physically?

CLIENT RESPONSE:

A 19-year-old woman named Lauren, diagnosed with bipolar disorder, drew a very large, bright red heart, which took up most of the page; she added lots of squiggly lines within it. Lauren stated that she has many mood changes throughout the day (e.g., the squiggles) but that she also has a big heart full of love and care. Lauren shared that she hopes people will overlook her moodiness and accept her the way she is because she has so much to share and give to others. Her fear was that her friends, especially her boyfriend, would leave her because of her mood disorder.

My Positive Traits

PROCEDURE: Create a drawing or collage symbolizing the characteristics that you admire about yourself, such as your strength, honesty, bravery, kindness, perseverance, or intelligence. Think about experiences you have had to endure and obstacles you have overcome.

BENEFITS: This exercise helps you acknowledge and examine your positive traits, especially those that you may have forgotten about or tend to overlook.

QUESTIONS FOR EXPLORATION:

1. What have you achieved over the years? Examples may include learning to drive a car, graduating from high school or college, or getting married.

2. What are your strengths? Perhaps you are a good friend, and you are thoughtful, honest, and kind.

3. Which traits did you include (or exclude) that you might not ordinarily acknowledge?

Recipe for Self-Compassion

PROCEDURE: Create a recipe for self-compassion, and then design a food dish that corresponds with this recipe. This dish can be anything that you would consider a special treat, including a cake or other type of dessert, an appetizer, or a main dish like spaghetti and meatballs. Your recipe may be as unique as you like. A sample recipe may include ingredients such as ½ cup of love, 2 tablespoons of not judging, 3 teaspoons of positive self-talk, etc.

BENEFITS: Reciting and utilizing these ingredients as often as possible will help you feel more content and compassionate toward yourself and others. Creating a food dish from this recipe will also remind you to indulge yourself because "You are worth it!"

QUESTIONS FOR EXPLORATION:

1. In what way is your recipe (and the treat you created) indicative of the way you care for yourself?

2. What are the three healthiest ways that you currently care for yourself?

3. What may stand in your way of treating yourself with compassion (e.g., not feeling worthy or lack of time)?

4. Have there been ways in which you cared for yourself in the past that you are neglecting nowadays?

Self-Soothing for Increased Well-Being

PROCEDURE: Create a piece of art that represents the ways in which you can soothe yourself. Examples may include taking a warm bubble bath, reading a favorite novel, drinking a hot cup of herbal tea, drawing or painting, or calling a friend.

BENEFITS: Permitting yourself to relax aids in stress reduction, facilitates peace of mind, and often increases motivation. It may also lower blood pressure and improve energy levels.

QUESTIONS FOR EXPLORATION:

1. What is the most effective way that you are currently self-soothing?

2. How often do you allow yourself to relax? Every day, periodically (a few times a week), rarely, or never?

3. What may stand in the way of your being self-compassionate?

4. In what way(s) would you like to self-soothe that you are not practicing now?

CLIENT RESPONSE:

A young woman named Ruthie drew a page full of dogs and shared that her two poodles give her much joy and love. She remarked that when she is depressed, they cuddle next to her, wriggle under the covers, and fall asleep with her. Ruthie said that her poodles seem to know what she needs, understand her moods, and accept her unconditionally. She remarked that her dogs are the only things in her life that provide happiness and help her feel less stressed.

Gift Box of Comfort

PROCEDURE: Design a box filled with ideas for gifts that you want and/or need to feel happier and comforted. Examples may include a new car, more money, a best friend, a good night's sleep, or peace of mind.

BENEFITS: Exploring your wants and needs will help you decide what you truly need to possess in order to be content. As you engage in this exploration, you may that realize you have more than enough or, perhaps, that you are missing key components of your life. If this is the case, then you may begin to examine ways to obtain what you believe will increase your life satisfaction. A plan of action may begin as soon as possible.

QUESTIONS FOR EXPLORATION:

1. What do you want or need now?

2. What have you wanted in the past that you now have in your possession? This can include a person, place, or thing.

3. If you were to have whatever you need, do you think this would change your life, mood, motivation, or behavior?

Shopping Cart of Compassion

PROCEDURE: Draw a shopping cart and fill it in with self-care items, such as books, love, coffee, hot cocoa, and friends. *The group leader may provide outlines of carts to participants who desire more structure.*

BENEFITS: Examining various ways to take care of yourself physically and emotionally is a first step toward making healthy lifestyle choices and changes.

QUESTIONS FOR EXPLORATION:

1. What is in your shopping cart? How full is it?

2. How can you relate your cart to your present self-help practices?

3. What would you place in a shopping cart for a friend or family member? Would it be similar to or different from your cart?

4. What is one thing you can start doing daily to take care of yourself?

Healing the Heart

PROCEDURE: Think about people, places, and things you need to heal. Then, create a collage or other piece of art representing what you need to feel better physically and emotionally. For example, perhaps you need family, love, health, children, the correct medicine, spirituality, and/or hope.

BENEFITS: This exercise raises self-awareness of needs and creates hope for the future by clarifying what makes, as per Marsha Linehan, a "life worth living." When we pursue our dreams and goals, we are generally happier, and our self-esteem increases. We are doing what we want to do and not what we believe others or society requires of us. In this manner, we are showing ourselves support, love and kindness. When we take time to nurture ourselves we allow ourselves to recover emotionally and physically, and as a result, we become increasingly strong and motivated.

QUESTIONS FOR EXPLORATION:

1. What items were added to your collage?

2. How important are those items to your healing process?

3. Are the items attainable? Are they realistic?

4. If the items are realistic and attainable, what is the plan of action to get them?

5. Have you ever had any of these items in your life before? If so, did they make your life more fulfilling?

CLIENT RESPONSE:

A 33-year-old woman named Nancy designed this collagette to symbolize gratitude and hope for a brighter future. Nancy stated that she needed to focus on gratitude for her family and friends instead of anger and resentment towards her ex-husband. She acknowledged that her anger was keeping her stuck, and the associated stress was beginning to negatively affect her physical health. Her migraines were becoming more frequent and more intense. She shared that before participating in this exercise she felt depressed and tired, and then she "woke up," when she began creating art. As she worked she felt more motivated, capable and energetic.

The Spirit in My Hands

PROCEDURE: Using a pencil, make an outline of both your hands and fill them in with colors, designs, words, and shapes that reflect your inner beauty. For example, your inner beauty may be considered kindness, honesty, and a love of humanity.

BENEFITS: We often focus on our negatives, which is detrimental to our self-esteem. This exercise provides you an opportunity to focus on your positive characteristics. You can explore your inner beauty instead of worrying if you are too short, too tall, too thin, or too fat. Appearances change, but inner beauty lasts a lifetime.

QUESTIONS FOR EXPLORATION:

1. What do your hands say about your strengths and positive qualities?

2. How is your inner beauty reflected in your design?

3. What helpful and positive things have your hands done over the years? For example, your hands may have bathed a baby, worked to earn money, baked a cake, cleaned a house, planted flowers, painted a picture, washed clothes, or soothed a broken heart.

CLIENT RESPONSE:

A 58-year-old man name Bert drew two large hands filled with tiny fish, alcohol bottles, and hearts. Bert was a joker and thought the fish, which were sketched in a comic-like style, "looked fishy." Bert remarked that he had worked hard throughout his life, but he also "played around a lot." He shared that he loved to go fishing and enjoyed preparing and cooking the catch of the day for his wife and family. He acknowledged that he was an excellent cook, inspired by his grandmother whom he adored.

Although he was able to admire his work ethic, he regretted his years of drinking, which caused his wife much stress and grief. The hearts symbolized his apologies to his family and his great love and admiration for his wife. He stated that he didn't know why she stood by him all these years. Bert shared that he was going to spend the rest of his life making up for his major mistakes and pledged to be a good husband and father.

Supporting Myself with Hugs I

PROCEDURE: Create a piece of art that illustrates the ways you can give yourself a hug. Your creation may be a realistic or abstract representation of a hug, such as a sketch of you hugging yourself, colorful shapes reaching out in a loving embrace, or a collage of people surrounding you in a warm, caring way. Your creation can also be a collage of photos that are soothing, such as puppies, kittens, or people smiling and celebrating.

BENEFITS: We can't always depend on others for support; we need to learn to self-soothe and hug ourselves. Giving yourself a pat on the back for a job well done is extremely important. We need to acknowledge our strengths and successes. Other people's praises are wonderful, but, ideally, they should be like icing on the cake. Our praise to ourselves *is* the cake!

QUESTIONS FOR EXPLORATION:

1. When was the last time you gave yourself a hug?

2. Are you "hug-worthy"? If not, how can you view yourself in a more positive light?

3. Which techniques can you use to soothe yourself? Are there new methods you might try in the future?

4. How does it help you emotionally and physically when you show yourself kindness?

CLIENT RESPONSE:

A young woman named Sandra drew a colorful heart with a gray circle in the middle of it, stating her personal hug would involve giving herself permission to change her mind. The gray circle represented her inability to say "no" to others. Sandra shared that when she commits to do something, she always has to see it through, even when it isn't in her best interest. She told group members that recently she promised to help a friend move, and even though she had felt ill, she still helped her anyway and then came down with the flu. Sandra also shared that she feels too guilty to refuse an invitation or a request to help out at work although she might be exhausted or have other plans. Sandra resolved to continue to focus on her needs as much as possible in the future.

Supporting Myself with Hugs II

PROCEDURE: Draw a personal hug. What would it look like in terms of artistic design? It may be depicted realistically (e.g., a figure hugging itself) or with shapes and forms, and with various types of cut paper.

BENEFITS: When you hug yourself, you show yourself love and compassion. You become more independent when you do not have to rely on others for support and warmth. You become your own best friend and are able to ease any physical and emotional pain on your own.

QUESTIONS FOR EXPLORATION:

1. How would you describe the hug you symbolized? Is it all encompassing or is it shallow? Is it full of movement and color?

2. Does the hug seem strong, weak, or moderate?

3. Are you able to feel the symbolic hug?

4. Do you comfort yourself when sad, lonely, or stressed? If so, what are some of the ways you help yourself feel better?

Self-Soothing Quilt

ADDITIONAL MATERIALS: Sequins, beads, scraps of material, and tissue paper.

PROCEDURE: Design a personal quilt that will keep you warm, safe, and covered with support. You may create a drawing or painting of a quilt, or you can make a collage using materials such as beads, tissue paper, sequins, magazine photos, and scraps of material. You can make your quilt look traditional by using separate squares to designate various portions of it, or it may be more unique and abstract.

BENEFITS: The self-soothing quilt can be considered a metaphor for self-compassion, support, and comfort. Designing and utilizing it may help you find peace of mind and freedom from self-judgment. You can keep your quilt with you in your thoughts, providing you with a way to focus on positive images and upbeat feelings throughout the day.

QUESTIONS FOR EXPLORATION:

1. How can you comfort yourself when you feel stressed or depressed?

2. Are there specific thoughts or affirmations, or a certain item, you can keep with you as a self-care reminder?

3. Have your self-soothing methods changed over time? What has been your most effective technique?

Suit of Armor

PROCEDURE: Create your own personal suit of armor that will keep you safe from your own criticisms and negative thoughts. The armor may appear realistic or abstract, and it may be drawn, painted, or designed using collage materials.

BENEFITS: Sometimes, we must develop a hard outer shell to defend ourselves from others, but, more frequently, we have to defend ourselves from our own severe judgments and negativity. We can be our own best friend, but, unfortunately, we can also be our own worst enemy. You can defend yourself from self-imposed negativity by:

- Maintaining awareness of negative thinking patterns, and then lessening them and/or transforming them into something more positive

- Giving yourself daily breaks from negativity

- Talking back to your harsh thoughts; don't allow them to control you

- Reciting positive affirmations

- Focusing on your strengths

QUESTION FOR EXPLORATION:

1. What type of armor did you create?

2. Is your armor strong or weak, thin or thick, permeable or impermeable, etc.?

3. Is there a specific thought or feeling that your suit needs to guard against?

4. How would you be affected if you wore your suit every day? Would the suit be easy or difficult to wear? Would it feel cumbersome?

5. Have you worn armor in the past? Has it been effective?

CLIENT RESPONSE:

One young man drew a smiling mouth filled with large, gray teeth and stated that his armor is his sarcasm. He shared that he jokes a lot and sometimes intimidates people with his wise cracks. He knew his personality kept him from forming real relationships but shared that he was not ready to take off his armor right now. He had to continue working on trust issues. When he was asked what kept *him* safe from *his own judgments*, he shared that he liked video games and playing them kept him from focusing on his own problems.

Understanding the Inner Bully

PROCEDURE: Draw what you believe your inner bully looks and/or feels like. Your inner bully is the voice in your head that criticizes you, says you are always wrong, tells you that you are not good enough, says you will never win, and doesn't forgive you for making mistakes. When you are finished, give your bully a name. Doing so will help you form a relationship and dialogue with your bully, which will help reduce its power over your thoughts, feelings, and behavior.

BENEFITS: Drawing your inner bully provides the opportunity to analyze it, talk back to it, and learn ways to control it. You can tame your inner bully by:

- Initially developing an awareness that your inner bully exists

- Not allowing your bully to dominate your thoughts, *not* giving it permission to visit

- Transforming negative thoughts into more positive thoughts

- Focusing on deep breathing and mindfulness

- Focusing on achievements and positive traits

- Defining success in your *own* terms and not other people's standards

- Not comparing yourself to others

- Asking yourself what you would say to a friend who was feeling badly and act accordingly

- Taking tiny steps toward achievable goals

- Defending yourself from this bully just the way you would defend a good friend from someone who was tormenting them

QUESTIONS FOR EXPLORATION:

1. What does your bully look like (e.g., size, shape, color, facial expression)?

2. Is it taking up a tiny portion of the page, part of the page, or most of the page?

3. Do you feel ready to confront your bully?

4. How does your bully harm you?

5. Are there any benefits to having a bully?

6. When was the last time your bully took over? How did you feel?

7. How long have you had this tormentor?

8. How do you think the bully developed?

9. How do you feed it (e.g., negative thinking, fear, self-criticism)?

10. Is there a time of day when your bully is most dominant?

11. Is there someone or something that triggers it?

12. What is one thing you can do today to defend yourself?

Gratitude to My Body

PROCEDURE: Express gratitude to your body. Draw, paint, or use magazine or personal photos to create a piece of art that reflects your appreciation for your body. Think about the appreciation you have for your heart, brain, legs, hands, face, and general health. Explore what your body does for you. For example, it allows you to love, feel, eat, express yourself, hear, smell, taste, relate to others, and appreciate nature.

BENEFITS: Many individuals spend a lot of time criticizing the size, shape, and appearance of their bodies instead of appreciating what their bodies do for them and how hard their bodies work to allow them to live, love, and function. This exercise reminds us to appreciate our strengths and abilities, and to be less critical of superficial matters pertaining to our outward presentation.

QUESTIONS FOR EXPLORATION:

1. How did you depict your body and how did you show thankfulness for it?

2. How has your body helped you in the past? For example, perhaps you ran a race and won, or maybe your body came through an operation with flying colors.

3. How do you generally express gratitude toward your body? Do you eat a balanced diet, get enough sleep, take medication as prescribed, or think positive thoughts?

4. How can you begin thinking in a more positive way toward your body and recognize its importance to your physical and emotional health?

We Are Multifaceted

PROCEDURE: *Distribute a template of a human form, or ask participants to outline a human figure taking up much of a 8.5 × 11 inch page.* Fill in the figure with anything that you feel represents who you are. This can include your thoughts, feelings, goals, hopes, personality traits, likes, dislikes, problems, achievements, memories, affirmations, favorite vacation spots, hobbies, interests, family, or partners. You can use descriptive words, draw images or symbols, or cut out magazine photos to create this self-representation.

BENEFITS: This exercise increases self-worth and fosters your ability to accept yourself as you are. When we realize that we "wear many different hats" and have many facets to our personality, we become more cognizant of our strengths and abilities, instead of focusing only on our perceived deficits.

QUESTIONS FOR EXPLORATION:

1. How do you view yourself?

2. Do you tend to label or categorize yourself?

3. Is that helpful or unhealthy?

4. How many "hats" do you wear? How many different roles do you play in your life (e.g., sister, friend, partner, mother)?

5. What positive characteristics do you see in yourself?

6. What, if anything, would you like to change about yourself?

7. What are your proudest achievements?

Mask with Scars

PROCEDURE: *Provide clients with a 3D or flat cardboard mask, or ask them to cut an oval shape from a piece of thin cardboard.* Create a mask that includes the scars you have accumulated over time. These may include physical scars (such as those from an operation or accident) or emotional scars (such as those from a loss, break-up, or missed opportunity). You may draw these scars or represent them using specific shapes, designs, colors, and words that are personal to you.[3,4]

BENEFITS: This exercise helps you appreciate and acknowledge that being a survivor is something to be proud of and to celebrate. Scars demonstrate that you have overcome obstacles in your life. Scars are the beauty marks of survivors.[5] This project gives you the opportunity to view your difficult experiences in a way that acknowledges what has occurred, and also gives praise to your strength and perseverance. You have dealt with pain and distress and survived.

QUESTIONS FOR EXPLORATION:

1. How does your mask represent the difficult experiences you have encountered?

2. How did you represent your scars, and how do you view them?

3. How do you feel about your mask? Do you see it as significant? Is it attractive or unattractive to you?

4. What do you admire most about the way you deal and have dealt with adversity?

5. Which scar(s) are you most proud of when reflecting on your mask?

18

CLIENT RESPONSE:

A 45-year-old woman named Athena created a red mask with a variety of scars representing operations, accidents, losses, and a pending divorce from her husband of 15 years. Teardrops symbolized the hurt and pain she had felt over the years. The red face represented anxiety and anger at her husband, who had been having a year-long affair with his co-worker. The hearts symbolized her ability to keep persevering and attempting to be kind to herself in spite of her challenges and traumas. Athena shared that her most significant scar was the loss of her sister two years ago, who died unexpectedly from a severe bout of the flu and sepsis.

Athena remarked that she alternates in how she views her scars; sometimes, she sees them as extremely ugly, and, other times, she sees them as heroic and beautiful. On this particular day, she was able to take pride in them and was pleased that she continued to work in therapy and elsewhere to help herself.

> "In Japan, broken objects are often repaired with gold.
> The flaw is seen as a unique piece of the object's history,
> which adds to its beauty. Consider this when you feel broken."
>
> – Unknown source

Compassion with Hot Chocolate

PROCEDURE: Draw a picture of a large mug, and then fill your mug part of the way with hot chocolate or another comforting beverage, such as green tea. *The group leader may also provide an outline of a mug to clients who desire more structure.* On top of your beverage, draw images and symbols of things that you can use to provide yourself with self-compassion – for example, placing whipped cream on top of hot chocolate for a special treat. These sources of support can include coping skills, positive thoughts, affirmations, and self-soothing activities (e.g., self-praise, getting enough sleep, hugging yourself, creating mandalas, taking frequent breaks throughout the day, exercising, listening to music).

BENEFITS: This exercise helps you identify ways to find comfort, reduce stress, relax, and self-soothe. Showing self-compassion via actions and positive thoughts helps us reduce stress, and become motivated, energized, and tolerant toward ourselves and others.

QUESTIONS FOR EXPLORATION:

1. How full is your mug? Is it partly full or brimming over the top with ideas for self-compassion?

2. Do you find the mug useful? Will you utilize it again?

3. Which coping techniques do you find most useful?

4. Are there self-soothing techniques you would like to try in the future that you are not currently practicing?

Hugs and Comfort Mandala

PROCEDURE: Give imaginary hugs to other members in the group by saying, "I hug you because…" and then completing the statement. *Group leaders should encourage each individual to share until everyone receives a hug.*[6] After you have given a virtual hug to everyone in the group, create a mandala that symbolizes your reactions to being hugged or to giving a hug.

BENEFITS: Hugging is a healthy way to show compassion to yourself and others. It increases self-esteem, self-love, and feelings of connection with others. By giving others virtual hugs and articulating their strengths, you are able to share positive thoughts with others in a meaningful manner. Creating mandalas further emphasizes the positive effects of this exercise, as it serves as a tangible reminder of your own value and your value to others.

QUESTIONS FOR EXPLORATION:

1. How does your mandala represent the feelings you experienced during the exercise?

2. Did you allow yourself to accept the virtual hugs? Does the mandala reflect that acceptance?

3. Did you prefer to give or receive the hugs, or were you comfortable (or uncomfortable) with both experiences?

4. Was it difficult to internalize the hugs? Was this feeling demonstrated in your artwork?

5. Which part of your mandala shows the most self-compassion? The least self-compassion?

Protective Boundary from Negativity

PROCEDURE: Draw a boundary that will help protect you from negative thoughts and demands, including the negativity that emanates from within and that which comes from others. Think about the reasons you need this boundary, and take into account its size, shape, color, design, and sturdiness.

BENEFITS: This exercise helps foster self-esteem, enhance feelings of safety and peace, and increase feelings of control. Creating your own protective boundary helps you come to the realization that you can deny the requests of others. It serves as a reminder that *your needs matter*.

QUESTIONS FOR EXPLORATION:

1. How would you describe the appearance of your boundary? Think about its size and intensity or lack thereof.

2. How long has the boundary been up? Does it seem effective?

3. How often, if ever, do worrisome feelings, ideas, or people get through the boundary?

4. What materials compose your boundary (e.g., wood, bricks, paper, concrete)?

5. Does the boundary help you or harm you?

6. Would you like to change or modify the boundary?

7. How much longer do you think you'll need it?

Inspiration on a Clothespin

ADDITIONAL MATERIALS: Clothespins, sequins, and small, flat beads.

PROCEDURE: Decorate a clothespin with permanent marker, and paint or write a positive word, phrase, or affirmation on it. You may add other tiny decorations to the clothespin as well, such hearts, flowers, sequins, etc. If there is extra time, place a coating of Mod Podge® over it for shine and protection. Next, cut out a photo, picture, word, or affirmation, and clip it in place using the clothespin as a unique personal holder.

BENEFITS: Viewing affirmations increases positive feelings and provides you with an incentive to engage in new experiences. The clothespin becomes an object of positivity; you may change the messages daily or whenever desired. Affirmations increase self-esteem and motivation because they serve as reminders of goals and positive traits.

QUESTIONS FOR EXPLORATION:

1. How does the way you decorated the clothespin relate to your current mood and energy level? How do the colors, designs, or decorations serve as a reflection of you?

2. Which affirmation, picture, or word did you choose to attach to the clothespin?

3. How can focusing on encouraging thoughts help you function more effectively and purposefully?

4. What time of day (and/or day of the week) would it be most helpful for you to read the affirmation(s) on the clothespin?

Exploration of Interlocking Arms

PROCEDURE: Draw a figure that represents yourself interlocking arms with one or more other figures.[8] As the artist, you decide distance, design, shading, color, etc.

BENEFITS: This exercise helps you focus on developing self-awareness regarding the support, warmth, closeness, and connections you have with others, which is so important for healing, hope, and motivation.

QUESTIONS FOR EXPLORATION:

1. How were the arms in your sketch interlocked? For instance, were they tightly knit together or stretched farther apart?

2. Was there emphasis on connection between the arms (e.g., using dark or colorful lines), or did the connection seem less important (e.g., perhaps the arms were lightly sketched)?

3. What does the symbol of interlocking arms mean for you? For example, for some people it means love, support, and a healthy closeness. However, for others, it might mean co-dependency or even a smothering of attention or affection.

4. Is there anyone with whom you feel a strong connection? Is that connection helpful? Does it inspire you in any way? For example, does it help you face each day and function even when you'd rather stay in bed or isolate from others?

CLIENT RESPONSE:

A 55-year-old woman named Sam sketched a dream that she had recently. She drew herself interlocking elbows with her beloved father, who had passed away a few years ago. In her dream, she was in her home, walking into her kitchen for a midnight snack. She and her father were both in pajamas, passing by each other as he was leaving the kitchen. They interlocked arms for a brief moment and then continued going their own way. Sam shared that it was a very quick interaction, but one that left her feeling loved and happy. She stated that when she woke up, she felt safe and peaceful, and immediately wrote about the dream in her journal. She believed the dream was a message from her father saying, "We will always be together, and I love you."

Self-Compassion Spiral

PROCEDURE: Create a full-page spiral and fill the concentric circles of the spiral with small images, phrases, or words that demonstrate ways to engage in positive self-compassion. Some examples of ways in which you can practice self-compassion include:

- Freely engaging in art without specific expectations

- Taking coffee, tea, or relaxation breaks

- Practicing saying the affirmation, "I am enough"

- Engaging in positive self-talk

- Encouraging yourself

- Practicing mindfulness

- Taking healthy risks

- Not judging yourself

- Allowing yourself to make mistakes

- Taking small steps toward goals

- Not comparing yourself to others

- Allowing yourself to be "imperfect"

BENEFITS: This exercise helps promote self-compassion by reminding you of the steps you can take to be kind to yourself, which can lead to better emotional and physical health, increased motivation, and improved attitude.

QUESTIONS FOR EXPLORATION:

1. What are the advantages of self-compassion?

2. Which techniques are prominent in your spiral?

3. Which techniques do you engage in now or would you like to pursue in the future?

CLIENT RESPONSE:

A 54-year-old woman named Anna created a colorful spiral, which she characterized as optimistic. She viewed her spiral as a circle of goals and stated that she was going to try to accomplish most of the goals she had included. In particular, she mentioned that she would try to exercise, be more positive, not judge herself, not compare herself to others, and get more sleep. Anna also stated that she would attempt to eat in a healthier manner, engage in hobbies like art, and appreciate her friends and family. She decided to hang the spiral on her refrigerator to remind her of her blessings and goals.

Elephant Filled with Self-Compassion

PROCEDURE: Draw the outline of an elephant, and then fill in the outline with small images, words, colors, and designs that represent ways you can show yourself self-compassion. You can also cut out magazine photos to create your self-compassion elephant. *The group leader can also distribute an outline of an elephant instead of asking clients to draw one.*

BENEFITS: Elephants are extremely intelligent animals that support each other and seem to be very intuitive toward themselves and others. They are strong, fearless, and protect their young and each other. They are positive role models that can teach us a lot about caring for ourselves and those around us. Therefore, the elephant serves as an appropriate focus for a self-compassion exercise. By creating your own self-compassion elephant, you can enhance your self-love, increase your confidence, and develop the motivation needed to take healthy risks and move forward.

QUESTIONS FOR EXPLORATION:

1. What feelings and thoughts are symbolized in your artwork?

2. Are you able to relate to the elephants in any way in terms of trust, intelligence, and support?

3. How does (or would) showing yourself compassion help you the most?

4. When was the last time you demonstrated compassion toward yourself? Did it improve your mood and/or change your behavior?

Doodles of Self-Love

PROCEDURE: Fill the page with curvy doodles, and then fill the shapes within the doodles with images and words that reflect everything that is positive about you. For example, you may include a face with a smile to symbolize your sense of humor, or a hand to symbolize your giving nature. In addition, add ways you can comfort and support yourself. Finally, fill in the remainder of the design with colors that reflect optimism and hope.

BENEFITS: The doodle design helps you mindfully focus on the positive aspects about yourself, including the ways in which you can use this self-love to increase feelings of self-worth and positivity, and combat feelings of depression and unworthiness.

QUESTIONS FOR EXPLORATION:

1. Which part of the design do you find most meaningful?

2. What do you admire most about yourself?

3. How often do you show yourself love and appreciation?

4. What are some of the ways you can treat yourself in a loving manner?

CLIENT RESPONSE:

Mary, a 51-year-old woman with bipolar disorder, added mostly hopeful and cheerful words and pictures to her design. She focused on joy, fun, and family to symbolize her desire to take it one day at a time and think about the things in her life "that really count." She stated that she wanted to be more positive and not worry so much. She mentioned that she stresses over everything, including the weather, what to wear, what to cook for dinner, and whether or not her husband loves her. She shared that her husband has to reassure her of his devotion many times a day or else she feels anxious to the point of being incapacitated. She fears that he will leave her and never return.

Mary also added the words "travel" and "escape" to represent her desire to escape from her illness and the slew of problems associated with it, and also to take a much-needed vacation. Mary mentioned that she hadn't taken a vacation in over 20 years. She stated that she enjoyed the project because it gave her the opportunity to reflect on her own wants and needs. She said she usually helps others but always feels guilty attending to herself; she feels she's not worthwhile and doesn't deserve special treatment because her illness causes her family so much grief and stress.

chapter two
mindfulness

Mindfulness is a practice that helps people experience peace and serenity. Although mindfulness has its origins in Eastern philosophy and Buddhism, individuals do not need to be religious or even spiritual to practice it. Rather, practicing mindfulness simply involves paying attention to what is happening in the present moment with intention and without judgment.[1] In particular, it involves non-judgmentally observing, describing, and participating fully in one thing at a time.

When you are mindful, you are fully aware of your senses and experiences. Because mindfulness is about observation without criticism, you don't judge any of your thoughts, feelings, or behaviors. Rather, you focus your full attention on what you are currently experiencing and let your incoming thoughts gently flow away without dwelling on them. In this respect, mindfulness is a skill that helps you "defuse" because it allows you to distance yourself from any unhelpful thoughts, feelings, or behaviors.[2] It allows you to catch negative thought patterns *as they occur* before you go into a downward spiral of catastrophic thinking.[3] It helps you be less reactive to what is happening in the moment and puts you back in control of your life.[4]

Research has shown that regularly practicing mindfulness can improve both mental and physical health. In particular, it has been shown to reduce anxiety, decrease obsessive thoughts, reduce pain, and help individuals find pleasure in life. Because mindfulness teaches individuals to let go of their worries and regrets, it helps them to more fully participate in and enjoy relationships and activities. It also increases self-esteem as individuals begin to worry less and less about what others think and, instead, start to regain a sense of control over their life.

There are a variety of practices that promote mindfulness, including deep breathing, focusing on the breath, observing one's thoughts, listening to music, and engaging in different forms of creative expression, such as creating a mandala or drawing a flower in detail. Art therapy in particular helps cultivate an attitude of mindfulness because being engaged in a creative endeavor helps individuals focus on the artwork itself. The artwork becomes their center of consciousness, and they become fully engaged in the experience – aware only of color, line, image, and design. They are not judging their work, but allowing their art to flow from within.

Storage for Wandering Thoughts

PROCEDURE: Draw a special place where you can store your worries and stressful thoughts. This special place could be a type of container or a specific location where you can temporarily hide your stressors, so you can take a well-deserved mental break. For example, you may choose to store these thoughts in an adorned box on top of your closet, in a brightly-colored container, in an old slipper kept under your bed, in a diary in your dresser drawer, in a jewelry box, in a safe, on a cloud, on a floating lily pad, in the middle of a forest, or in the recesses of your mind.

BENEFITS: One major benefit of mindfulness involves allowing our unwelcome thoughts to gently float away so that we can focus on what is happening now. Visualizing a place to keep unwanted thoughts helps us let them go, and it allows us to feel more focused and peaceful. When you imagine that your worries are concealed, you have the opportunity to take a breath and relax. With practice, this exercise may become a valuable coping technique. Everyone deserves a vacation from stress.

QUESTIONS FOR EXPLORATION:

1. Describe the location or container you have chosen to store your thoughts. What does it look like (e.g., size, shape, color)?

2. Describe its usefulness as a way to reduce stress.

3. When and where do you think you will most likely need to use this storage system?

4. Is there a particular time of day or day of the week when this thought storage container or location will be most helpful?

5. How are you currently handling troubling thoughts that tend to stay with you for a prolonged period of time?

This Mindful Moment

ADDITIONAL MATERIALS: Pipe cleaners and feathers.

PROCEDURE: Draw or paint everything you can think of that is taking place in your immediate environment right now. Think about what you are thinking, seeing, hearing, smelling, touching, and perhaps even tasting. You may use markers, pastels, crayons, and an array of textures to convey your surroundings, such as crumpled paper, pom-poms, pipe cleaners, or feathers.

BENEFITS: This mindfulness technique helps stop you from dwelling on your problems and worrying about what happened in the past or what might happen in the future. Focusing on your senses and immediate environment grounds you and enhances feelings of peace and tranquility.

QUESTIONS FOR EXPLORATION:

1. How can focusing attention on your surroundings help you feel more at ease?

2. Did you notice a difference in your stress level after working on this exercise?

3. How many items, sounds, thoughts, and sights did you include in your artwork?

4. Which of your senses do you think will be most useful when you want to reduce anxiety? For instance, would it involve your sense of hearing (e.g., listening to music), sense of touch (e.g., petting your dog or cat), or sense of taste (e.g., eating a piece of chocolate)?

Sacred Space for Stress Relief

PROCEDURE: A sacred space is one that is distinguished from other spaces. The rituals that people either practice at this place or direct toward it mark its sacredness and differentiate it from other defined spaces.[5] In this art therapy exercise, you will view a sacred place as one that is safe, divine, and personal. This space can be a place of worship, or it can be a place in your home, such as your bedroom or even an old, beloved chair that you find comforting. It can be a beautiful area in a park, at the beach, at a lake, or a soothing place in the recesses of your mind. Draw or paint your sacred place in any way you wish, using whatever materials that will help you represent your thoughts.

BENEFITS: Having a sanctuary, especially in times of stress, sadness, and hardship, can help you better cope with your current circumstances. It provides a relief and refuge that allows you to take a breath, self-soothe, calm yourself, and become better focused.

QUESTIONS FOR EXPLORATION:

1. What does your sanctuary look like? Describe its color, shape, size, and design.

2. Does it have any remarkable features?

3. Is it a place you have been to or is it a place you have just designed in your mind?

4. When do you think you will utilize this haven?

Mandaloodle for Mindful Expression

A mandaloodle is a mandala/doodle. It is a circle filled with a variety of shapes, lines, and figures that connect and blend together to create a personal design. Most of the lines and shapes tend to be small and detailed. Although a mandaloodle can be created with colors, it is usually black and white so the artist can readily follow the flow of the design. There is no right or wrong way to create a mandaloodle because the idea is to allow the design to evolve by connecting the lines and shapes in any way that the artist desires. If the artist is not satisfied with one shape, then another may overlap or be joined in such a way to change the original form into something else.

A mandaloodle represents change and the flow of life. It demonstrates how we can continue to form new ideas and increase creativity in our life. We can make lemonade out of lemons and transform or reinvent ourselves as our circumstances change. The focus on the mandaloodle is to be in the moment – to be mindful and "let our thoughts roll."

PROCEDURE: Using a paper plate, make an outline of a circle to form a mandala, and then begin creating and connecting doodles within the circle, beginning from any point within the circle.

BENEFITS: This is an enjoyable exercise that facilitates mindfulness and reduces stress by providing a healthy distraction from daily concerns. By drawing detailed lines in the mandala, the focus of your attention is brought to the experience of creating the mandaloodle, as opposed to fixating on past, present, or future concerns. The exercise also aids in problem solving and enhances creative thinking as you must work through mistakes by creating new images and shapes as the mandaloodle progresses.

QUESTIONS FOR EXPLORATION:

1. Were you able to give yourself permission to make mistakes and then use the lines to create new forms and images?

2. How does your mandaloodle reflect your mood and motivation?

3. Which lines catch your eye the most? Are there any parts of the design that you would like to change?

Reflections in My Hand Zendoodle

PROCEDURE: Outline your hand(s) as many times as you like, and fill in the hand outlines with doodles and affirmations. The doodles and affirmations may relate to goals, positive thoughts and feelings, or whatever is most pertinent in your life now. You may use black marker for a bold effect or a variety of colors for a brighter appearance.

BENEFITS: Self-awareness, stress reduction, and mindfulness are enhanced by focusing, being spontaneous, and expressing immediate thoughts and positive feelings.

QUESTIONS FOR EXPLORATION:

1. How does being in the moment affect your mood and concentration?

2. In which ways does your design represent your thoughts or personality characteristics?

3. In which ways does your hand drawing represent what is occurring in your mind and body? For example, a chaotic design may represent inner turmoil; or from a medical perspective, swollen fingers and cold hands may be signs of lupus or other immune system disorders.

CLIENT RESPONSE:

Jamie, a 35-year-old woman recovering from depression, created a unique hand zendoodle. She shared that she needed to be more mindful and hoped this exercise might help remind her to be in the moment. Her favorite part of the design was writing "I am enough" by the outline of her wrist because she stated, "I never feel I am good enough." Jamie stated that she always feels "behind everyone else" and "left out." She remarked that all her friends from school have good jobs and professions, but she is just a volunteer who often doesn't have the energy to even get out of bed in the morning. Jamie said she liked the doodle part of the design because there were no expectations.

Cat on Head Exercise

PROCEDURE: Place a piece of drawing paper on your head and spend a few minutes drawing a cat with your dominant hand. Next, place another sheet of paper on your head and draw a cat again with your non-dominant hand. In both instances, you are drawing the cat while the paper is being balanced on your head. After you have finished your drawings, share your work with the group and discuss your thoughts and feelings about the exercise.[6] *Another option is to divide group members into pairs while drawing, and afterward, have each pair discuss their thoughts and reactions with their partner.* When sharing your work and commenting on the work of others, try not to judge the work – only make objective observations, such as, "I notice a black line under the nose" or "There are eyes placed above the head."

BENEFITS: This activity increases mindfulness, self-awareness, connectedness, non-judgmental attitudes, and fun. Group members feel connected to one another through sharing, supporting one another and laughing together. There are few expectations of skilled artwork, so most people allow themselves to be spontaneous and take healthy risks, which can be generalized and used for therapeutic discussion (e.g., taking healthy risks in life such as applying for a new job, learning a skill, or making new friends).

QUESTIONS FOR EXPLORATION:

1. What were you thinking about during this exercise? Were you in the moment?

2. What were the discernible differences between the sketches drawn with your dominant and non-dominant hand?

3. Were you able to be non-judgmental when describing your artwork and asking questions about the other pictures?

4. Did you find yourself comparing yourself to others (e.g., thinking, "Her work is more skilled than mine")?

5. Were you relaxed during the exercise or did you feel pressured?

6. Were you able to allow your work to be less than perfect?

Art's Path

PROCEDURE: Create a piece of art by letting your hand lead the way without conscious thought. Use markers, crayons, or pastels to create an intuitive design that develops from within. Try not to judge your work, but also try not to "judge your judging."

BENEFITS: This exercise helps with mindfulness, relaxation, stress reduction, and expression of feelings and emotions. Spontaneity, introspection, and thinking outside the box are enhanced when we give ourselves permission to express ourselves freely.

QUESTIONS FOR EXPLORATION:

1. Which feelings are elicited when you observe your artwork?

2. Does your artwork represent you in some way (e.g., personality, mood, or thoughts)?

3. Were you able to "just let go" as you were drawing?

4. Are you able to view your art without judging it?

5. Do you tend to criticize yourself, or do you allow yourself to be human, make mistakes, and stumble at times?

> "See where the art leads you."
>
> – Susan Buchalter

Painting with Tissue Paper to Reduce Stress

ADDITIONAL MATERIALS: Tissue paper that "bleeds" (can be found at an art supply store) and a base (e.g., heavy duty paper, such as watercolor paper, or small canvases work well).

PROCEDURE: Tear or cut colorful tissue paper into a variety of small, irregular pieces. You may do this beforehand or as you are working. Place one piece of tissue paper at a time on the base and brush it with water. You may see the colors begin to bleed, which will lead to attractive effects. Keep repeating this pattern of working until a pleasing design is formed. Allow the paper to dry a few minutes. Peel the tissue paper off the base to see your art come to life. You may leave the design as is or add doodles, affirmations, and other images using markers or paint.

BENEFITS: This is an enjoyable and freeing creative experience that helps you learn how to "go with the flow" and freely express your ideas, moods, and feelings. It can also reduce stress as you are given the opportunity to nonverbally express and release both positive and negative emotions through the use of color, design, image, and shape. This art technique may also be used to create mandalas or journals.

QUESTIONS FOR EXPLORATION:

1. In which ways does your design reflect your current mood?

2. Do you notice any eye-catching or meaningful images, shapes, or forms in your artwork?

3. Did you decide to add additional pictures or words to the design?

4. How did you feel while working in this spontaneous manner?

5. Were you able to allow yourself to relax and let your art evolve?

6. Does the way you approached this project relate in any way to the way you approach endeavors at home and at work?

Resting Mind and Serenity

PROCEDURE: Draw your mind at rest. You may include whatever images, shapes, and forms appear to you as you relax. Depict the calmness and peacefulness associated with being mindful.

BENEFITS: A calm mind helps you feel peaceful, stronger, and more focused. It gives you a respite from the trials of everyday life.

QUESTIONS FOR EXPLORATION:

1. What types of shapes, images, and colors were used to portray your mind?

2. Describe the way your mind usually works (e.g., calm, chaotic, swirling thoughts, negative thoughts, positive thoughts, confused, focused).

3. How can being mindful contribute to a calmer and happier life?

4. What does mindfulness mean to you?

5. What part of your life or lifestyle would benefit the most from being mindful?

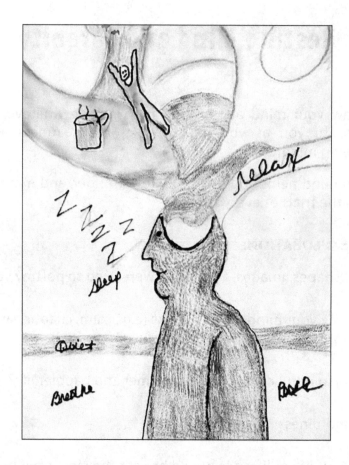

CLIENT RESPONSE:

James, a 39-year-old veteran challenged with PTSD and addiction issues, drew his desire to relax and calm his chaotic mind. James shared he wished he could experience serenity and a restful night's sleep instead of his usual fragmented four hours of sleep per night. He stated he had vivid dreams and nightmares, which were often terrifying. He remarked that he frequently wakes up in the middle of the night sweating profusely and finding it difficult to breathe.

James explained that he attempts to relax as much as possible before bedtime, even sipping warm milk, and listening to guided imagery and meditation CD's. He stated he imagines himself reclining under a shade tree, enjoying a warm, sunny spring day, but after a short while his mind wanders, and he ends up spiraling into a state of anxiety and confusion. He pledged that he was going to try yoga and create art more often, hoping drawing and painting would help him unwind and focus in a more mindful manner.

Intuitive Collagette

PROCEDURE: Browse through magazines and cut out photos that speak to you in some way. You may choose photos that you find attractive, unusual, stimulating, appealing, or unappealing. There doesn't have to be a specific reason for selecting the pictures. Try not to judge your selections. Next, glue the photos on a sheet of paper in any way you wish in order to create a personal collagette. You may then add strips of paper, paint, stickers, foam pieces, sequins, glitter, or other bits of collage materials to your artwork.

BENEFITS: This exercise helps enhance creativity, abstract thinking, and mindfulness because you are going with the flow and, most importantly, trying not to criticize your artistic talents or decision-making skills. Rather, you are choosing designs that intuitively speak to you without judging or questioning your decision.

QUESTIONS FOR EXPLORATION:

1. What is your reaction to the design?

2. Does your collagette, or part of it, convey a message to you?

3. Are you noticeably represented in the collagette? For example, does the inclusion of a figure resemble you in some way (e.g., your facial features, hair, body stance)?

4. Does your artwork encourage you to think about objectives or hopes for the future?

5. Are current problems or issues represented in your artwork?

6. Do you notice symbolic thoughts or feelings?

7. What would you title this artwork? Does the title relate directly to the collagette or to something else that you are currently experiencing?

CLIENT RESPONSE:

A 24-year-old woman named Sofia shared that she enjoyed working on this eye-catching collagette. She said that it reminded her to try to be more positive. The focal point of her collagette – a watch – symbolized her hopes for a successful career as a veterinarian. The watch, according to Sofia, was very expensive and related to her hopes for financial success and freedom. She added the word "dogs" and a Snoopy sticker to represent her love of dogs and all other animals. A slide and happy face stickers symbolized a relatively enjoyable childhood, although her parents divorced when she was seven years old.

Sofia remarked that she enjoyed working on the collagette base, which consisted of tissue paper and glue. She derived much satisfaction and a "sort of release" from tearing and gluing the small, colorful sheets of tissue paper. Sofia smiled and wondered aloud why her art seem so cheerful when she generally felt stressed and depressed. She did share that art therapy was her favorite group and that it lifted her spirits.

Mindful Observation Mandala

PROCEDURE: Draw the outline of a circle to create a mandala, and then draw an eye in the center of the mandala. Alternatively, you may cut out a photo of an eye from a magazine and glue it into the mandala. Next, draw what you see in your environment. This can include abstract symbols that are present in your surroundings (e.g., love, peace, happiness), as well as concrete objects (e.g., flowers, birds, trees, houses, people).

BENEFITS: Your self-awareness and senses become enhanced when you broaden your attentiveness and appreciation of your environment. By attending to what is happening in the here-and-now, you can reduce anxiety, learn to be "in the moment," and become increasingly grounded.

QUESTIONS FOR EXPLORATION:

1. How was your sensory awareness increased during this exercise?

2. What does your mandala convey about your surroundings?

3. Did you notice anything represented in your artwork that you might normally take for granted?

4. What is most beautiful or unique about your mandala and/or your current setting?

CLIENT RESPONSE:

Meg, a 38-year-old woman challenged with bipolar disorder, shared that she found this exercise calming as well as enjoyable. She first filled in the mandala with green watercolor paint and then used magazine photos to create the overall design. She was allowed to work throughout the session, even during a guided meditation exercise, because she found the project so healing.

Meg remarked she was able to quiet her mind as she studied what she viewed in the art room, and when she searched for specific objects in the magazines provided. She shared that she focused on things she saw indoors and outdoors, but she liked centering on group members the best because she found everyone so unique, especially one woman who appeared to be in a deep, meditative state. Meg shared she noticed that most participants appeared focused and friendly. Their positive attitudes helped her stay involved and feel comfortable.

The Trixie Doodle

PROCEDURE: Draw a Trixie, which looks like a cephalopod or tadpole that is usually created by children at about 2-4 years of age. The Trixie consists of a large circular head with two dots for eyes, and stick arms and legs emanating from the head. If you desire, you may choose to add a few extra features to the face to express your current mood.[7]

BENEFITS: The Trixie is a lighthearted, mindful reminder to breathe, relax, and allow the child within to emerge so you can freely express yourself without fear of being judged or stymied because of societal rules. It reminds you to focus on the here-and-now and to not dwell on the past or the future. The Trixie can make you smile and lift your mood, even if it is just for a few thoughtful moments. Whenever you feel anxious, you can draw a quick Trixie as a way to unwind, put life in perspective, and remind yourself to perhaps not take yourself so seriously.

QUESTIONS FOR EXPLORATION:

1. What does your sketch represent for you? Can you relate in any way to the Trixie?

2. How can drawing the Trixie relieve stress and bring about the playful part of your personality?

3. Are you able to allow yourself to play without fear of being judged or without judging yourself?

4. When was the last time you gave yourself permission to be spontaneous and creative?

CLIENT RESPONSE:

Tom (who is a female-to-male trans person), age 21, was thinking about changing his gender permanently but still had trepidation about such a dramatic change. He designed a gender-divided "Trixie" and joked that this figure appeared happy because it could be whatever it wanted to be. "He just walks around half man and half woman; he can decide each day what he wants to wear and how he wants to behave." When asked, he remarked that this sketch made him feel positive because it gave him hope for the future.

He ideally viewed a future where no one would care about what gender or sex a person was attracted to, and that people's "minds regarding these issues could be changed freely" without fear of prejudice or harm. Right after the group ended, Tom told me that he still wasn't sure whether he liked men, women, or both, and he stated that he sometimes felt very confused. He shared that life had been confusing for him since kindergarten.

Breath, Anxiety, and Mindfulness

PROCEDURE: When you find that your anxiety is escalating and your breath is becoming more intense than usual, make a sketch of your breathing pattern. Notice the force and pattern of your breathing, and symbolize it with color, shape, line, and design. Observe the way you press down with the crayon, pencil, or marker. Is the pressure light, moderate, or strong? Follow the flow of your breath and gradually begin to change the intensity of your art, working in accordance with your breathing pattern as it becomes shallower. Next, transform your "breath drawing" into a piece of art that represents positivity, peace, or strength. For example, you might transform the curving or chaotic "breath lines" into a bouquet of flowers or waves rolling gently onto a beach where people are enjoying the sun and surf.[8]

BENEFITS: This exercise facilitates stress reduction as you develop the ability to control anxiety and transform it into something calming and more positive. It may become a go-to exercise you choose to utilize periodically before worry and apprehension spiral into a full-blown anxiety attack.

QUESTIONS FOR EXPLORATION:

1. What type of design did you draw?

2. How does your design reflect your anxiety and its creative transformation?

3. Did focusing on your breath and then sketching your breath help you become calmer? Did your heart rate slow down?

4. Was there a significant difference between the first part of your drawing and the end result? What is your reaction to the completed picture? What would you title it?

Art Emptying

PROCEDURE: Without giving it much thought, begin drawing whatever images, shapes, figures, or doodles come to mind until the paper is filled or almost filled.

BENEFITS: This exercise facilitates an attitude of mindfulness as you allow yourself to be spontaneous and create a meaningful work of art without worrying about ability, intent, making mistakes, or failing. You are just allowing yourself "to be."

QUESTIONS FOR EXPLORATION:

1. How did it feel to be in the moment "creatively"?

2. Did you allow yourself to go with the flow?

3. Do you allow yourself to be spontaneous in your everyday life?

4. Do you take healthy risks or generally play it safe?

5. How important is it for you to occasionally "let go" and be playful and free?

Create Your Mantra

A mantra is a commonly repeated word or phrase, especially in advocacy or for motivation.[9] *It can also involve a series of phrases or words that are sung or chanted in the context of meditation. A mantra is more than just a repeated word or phrase, as the energy created by singing or chanting the mantra is intended to help individuals achieve their goals. Examples of mantras include: "I am enough," "I deserve love in my life," "I will feel the fear and do it anyway," and "I will trust in the process of my life."*[10]

PROCEDURE: Choose a personal mantra and then illustrate it any way you please. You may draw or paint any images that come to mind while reciting your mantra, or you may illustrate its meaning or the feeling it evokes in you. You may also use realistic pictures, abstractions, and/or magazine photos to illustrate your mantra.

BENEFITS: Mantras calm the mind, improve immunity, and help release stress. They give the wandering mind a focal point toward which to channel energy.[11] By creating your own personal mantra, you can increase motivation, self-awareness, and self-esteem.

QUESTIONS FOR EXPLORATION:

1. What is the relationship between your illustration and your mantra?

2. How does your mantra help you feel motivated?

3. What is most significant about your mantra?

4. When are you most likely to use your mantra?

Mindfulness Stone for Self-Expression

ADDITIONAL MATERIALS: White or light-colored stones, permanent markers, brushes, magazines, glue sticks, Mod Podge.

PROCEDURE: *Group leaders should give clients a small stone suitable for painting or collage work.* On the small stone in front of you, write a saying, create a drawing, or glue small pictures that remind you to slow down and stay in the moment. For example, a photo of a rose may remind you to stop and smell the roses. Similarly, the phrase "Take it one day at a time" or the word "Now" can remind you to live in the moment. After you have finished decorating your stone, cover it with Mod Podge and let it dry a few hours. This will keep the photos and words from peeling and give the stone a sheen.

BENEFITS: This exercise helps you cultivate an attitude of mindfulness by reminding you to stay in the here-and-now. The use of affirmations can help you feel motivated and broaden your thinking. You may choose to use the stone as a paperweight or carry it around with you as a reminder to relax and not judge yourself or others.

QUESTIONS FOR EXPLORATION:

1. Which mindful affirmation was placed on your stone?

2. How will the stone help you stay focused, upbeat, and motivated?

3. How might having a tangible object to hold on to and view help inspire you to keep focused, determined, and calm?

Garden of Reflection

PROCEDURE: Draw a garden, making sure to include a variety of items that you might find, such as birds, butterflies, squirrels, bees, and greenery (e.g., trees, bushes, flowers). Place a small spiral next to every item in the garden that you find serene. When you are done, review your drawing, taking time to concentrate on the spiraled points while breathing in and out slowly and mindfully.

BENEFITS: This activity promotes mindfulness, stress reduction, and practice focusing on the senses. The garden imagery reminds us to "stop and smell the roses," and to be mindful of our environment and the beauty of life.

QUESTIONS FOR EXPLORATION:

1. What is special about the garden?

2. Is it a place you'd like to visit?

3. Which part of the garden do you find most relaxing?

4. Which of your senses do you tend to concentrate on the most while trying to unwind in a place like your garden?

Mindful Observation and Awareness

PROCEDURE: Chose an object or scene and imagine that you are viewing it for the very first time. Draw every aspect of it in detail, including how it makes you feel and how it arouses your senses. For example, you may choose to draw a flower, an orange, snow, a wooded forest, a lush park or garden, or the seashore.

BENEFITS: This exercise helps to facilitate relaxation, enhance concentration, and increase awareness of your surroundings and the beauty in our environment. It helps us look at the world with an attitude of openness, newness, and awe.

QUESTIONS FOR EXPLORATION:

1. Which details did you observe that you might have missed if you weren't fully engaged in this exercise?

2. Were you able to focus solely on the object or scene you were drawing?

3. How can mindfulness help you appreciate life and increase gratitude?

4. What is one way you can use your senses to make mundane chores and responsibilities less taxing?

The Sun as Imagery
for Serenity

PROCEDURE: *Read the following guided imagery to group members while they sit in a comfortable position with their eyes closed. Then, ask clients to draw any feelings derived from the guided imagery experience, such as the sensations of healing, peace, or the warmth of the sun.*

"Imagine you are reclining in a soft hammock in a lush, lovely garden. It's a warm, beautiful day, and you are feeling at peace. The birds are softly chirping, and there is a slight breeze. The fragrance of wild flowers and roses permeates the air. As you begin to drift into a light slumber, you can feel the soothing warmth of the sun emitting its rays down on you. The rays are slowly spreading through all parts of your body: your forehead, eyes, nose, mouth, neck, shoulders, back, arms, hands, fingers, chest, stomach, legs, feet, and toes. Feel the healing warmth and soothing comfort the sun provides. It envelops you in a cocoon of love and serenity. You can feel yourself healing and at peace with the world. Take a few more minutes to relax and take in this scenery, and when you are ready, you can come back to the room, open your eyes, and take a few deep breaths."

BENEFITS: This guided imagery promotes stress reduction and self-soothing by allowing your mind to go to a place of comfort and healing. It is one of many relaxation techniques you can use to lessen anxiety and heal the psyche and soul.

QUESTIONS FOR EXPLORATION:

1. How does your artwork depict the feelings you experienced while listening to the imagery?

2. Were you able to focus on what was being said or did you find yourself distracted?

3. Which part of the imagery did you find most soothing?

4. Do you think you will be able to use images in your artwork as visual cues to help reduce stress at home?

Spiritual Journey

PROCEDURE: Draw your spiritual journey. You may interpret your spiritual journey in any way you wish. Spirituality itself can involve a strong connection you have with nature, art, religion, or anything very special that brings you meaning and creates a special place in your heart and soul. In essence, it involves a sense of connection to something bigger than yourself and is a universal aspect of the human experience.[12]

You can symbolize your spiritual journey by depicting your life path, inner and outer self, or quest for understanding and awakening to the "real you." It can also include a representation of the various beliefs you have or are contemplating, ways in which you are growing emotionally, problems and obstacles you are encountering, the process of understanding yourself and your environment, or your quest to find inner solace and peace with the world.

BENEFITS: Developing a connection with something larger than yourself can help bring you a sense of peace, hope, and acceptance, particularly in times of difficulty. By becoming acquainted with the beliefs that give you meaning, you can widen your view of yourself and the world and gain a greater understanding regarding the importance of perspective. It can also help you realize that you have the power of choice, which can motivate you to engage in actions that align with your beliefs.

QUESTIONS FOR EXPLORATION:

1. What does your journey look like?

2. What message is your journey relaying to you?

3. What do you notice on your journey that is positive and/or negative?

4. How have you or will you cope with any bumps or roadblocks on your journey?

5. Is your journey long and drawn out? Is it a lifelong process?

6. What responsibility are you taking on this quest?

7. Will you accept help if needed?

8. Are you looking to transform yourself or your way of thinking in any way?

9. Are you gaining wisdom and knowledge?

Mindful Coloring Design

PROCEDURE: Create a coloring outline of a serene scene or comforting object that you can use as a coloring page. For example, you may choose to draw the outline of a beach scene, a flower, ocean waves, or any other tranquil scene that comes to mind. *The group leader will make copies of the outlines and put together a booklet containing all of the group members' work, which will be distributed during the next session. Each client will receive their own coloring book that they can use to use to reduce stress, focus, and be mindful.*

BENEFITS: Many people greatly enjoy filling in coloring outlines. They find it pleasant, relaxing, and it helps them distract from worries. Designing your own outlines makes the experience more creative and meaningful, and it aids in problem solving and abstract thinking as you work to develop your own designs. This exercise also enhances self-esteem as you are able to watch others relax and benefit from filling in *your own* unique outlines.

QUESTION FOR EXPLORATION:

1. How does your artwork convey a feeling of peace?

2. How do you feel about sharing your art with others?

3. How might focusing on your outline help you and/or others feel more tranquil?

4. In addition to engaging in art, what are some other ways you can achieve serenity (e.g., deep breathing, yoga)?

CLIENT RESPONSE:

Clients seemed to enjoy this project, and they were particularly pleased with the coloring pamphlet created and distributed to group members. Although filling in coloring outlines is not considered art therapy, the creative process that went into designing the outlines themselves is very healing and therapeutic. Many participants designed at least two outlines and wanted to work on more at home. The clients appeared gratified that they were being acknowledged for their artwork and contributing to other group members' enjoyment and well-being.

Sketching a Prayer

PROCEDURE: Draw a personal prayer that you find inspiring and comforting. It may be a prayer related to health, hope, love, family, or change. It does not need to be religious at all in nature, and it can be a prayer to a higher power, the earth, the universe, a loved one, or yourself. Think about colors, design, and meaning as you draw. Words and phrases may be added as well.

BENEFITS: Praying provides us with a sense of hope, support, solace, and control by allowing us to put into words that which we desire, wish for, or need. Some people feel that they have more power by praying, as they believe that their prayers will be answered in some way by a superior power or being, or the universe.

QUESTIONS FOR EXPLORATION:

1. What is special about your personal prayer? What part of your imagery strikes you the most?

2. Did you find it helpful to illustrate your prayer? Did it help clarify your thoughts? Was it soothing?

3. How might prayer help you in times of trouble, stress, illness, or sadness?

4. Do you believe that your prayers have ever been answered in some way? Have you ever been instrumental in answering your own or someone else's prayers?

Brushing Away Negative Thoughts

PROCEDURE: *Group leaders should read the following guided imagery to clients while they sit in a comfortable position with their eyes closed:*

"Close your eyes and take a few deep breaths, in through your nose and out through your mouth. Make yourself comfortable, relax your body, and sit so that your feet are planted firmly on the floor. Imagine that you are in a safe, peaceful place. It can be a place you have visited before or someplace new. It can be real or imaginary. All that matters is that you feel peaceful and safe there.

Listen thoughtfully to any sounds in this new environment, such as birds tweeting, leaves rustling in the breeze, a cricket chirping, or perhaps a cicada buzzing somewhere nearby. Visualize the sights, colors, forms, and shapes. Do you see a rainbow in the air, a deep blue sea, a winding river, puffy white clouds gently floating overhead, or perhaps a vast garden filled with multicolored blooms? Feel the breeze in the air and the sun's nourishing rays sending luxurious warmth on and within you. Inhale the freshness of country air, or maybe the salty sea air near an expanse of a picturesque beach, or perhaps the luscious scents of a field filled with wildflowers.

Allow your body to relax and be at one with this special place. Let any negative or stressful thoughts gently drift away. Now visualize a large paintbrush and choose the most soothing color in your artist palette. Is it a light pastel pink, a soothing seafoam green, or maybe a deep-sea blue? Fill your brush with a generous amount of your chosen color, and begin painting on an imaginary canvas, brushing away all annoying, stressful, and unhealthy thoughts so that you are covering them up one by one, brushing away all fear, worry, and anxiety. When your mental canvas is clear, and only composed of the one soothing color, sit with it for a few minutes. Your mind is now a blank canvas, so relaxing, so relaxing.

Next, you are going to create a new canvas. A canvas that *you* will control; you will be the artist of your thoughts. Visualize, once again, a pleasing, serene place. Think about the colors, scenery, landscape, and people or animals that may be included there. Enjoy designing the setting and visualize yourself there. Re-create the scene as needed until you feel perfectly at ease in this new environment, attentively viewing it and enjoying it.

Now open your eyes, take a few deep, cleansing breaths, stretch, and come back to the room, allowing yourself to acclimate for a few minutes. Next, draw this soothing place in any way you please. Just allow your hands and heart to lead the way. Please do not judge your work; focus on freely expressing yourself and remaining mindful of the experience."

BENEFITS: This guided imagery reminds you to be the artist of your life canvas. You have the ability to choose much of what happens in your environment, and you have the ability to choose how you react to life events. By coming to this recognition, you can better cultivate an attitude of mindfulness in your everyday life, which will reduce feelings of stress and increase feelings of control.

QUESTIONS FOR EXPLORATION:

1. What type of place did you choose to draw? Is it realistic or imaginary?

2. How would you feel, or how would things be different, if you were there now? For example, would your mood be different? Would your life or relationships change in some way?

3. What stressful or unhealthy things did you "brush over"? Was it something in particular, such as a specific event? Was it a mood, feeling, person, place, thing, or illness?

4. How did you feel when you brushed over your stress? Was it freeing and cathartic? Or did it produce some anxiety or apprehension?

Inner Peace Collagette

ADDITIONAL MATERIALS: Construction paper, scissors, glue, and various collage materials (e.g., magazines, pom-poms, feathers, sequins, a variety of textiles, glitter).

PROCEDURE: Take a few deep breaths, close your eyes, and listen to tranquil music for a few minutes. *Group leaders should play a soothing musical track for this exercise, such as "Tranquil Guitar CD - Soothing Music For Relaxation, Meditation and Sleep" by Ryan Judd - Board Certified Music Therapist (sold by: The Rhythm Tree), or "50 Classics For Relaxation (2 CD)" (sold by: ThriftTaco).* As you listen to the music, relax your body and try to free your mind from all other thoughts. Once the song(s) is finished playing, create a collagette that represents the peace you felt while listening to the music.

BENEFITS: This self-soothing exercise reduces stress and promotes peaceful thoughts and feelings, which are further reinforced through the symbolism that is represented in the collagette. You can return to this feeling of peace and serenity whenever you want by looking back at your collagette.

QUESTIONS FOR EXPLORATION:

1. What did you visualize while engaging in the exercise?

2. How relaxed did you feel? How does your art reflect your feelings of tranquility?

3. What are your other self-soothing techniques? Which ones are most effective?

Mindful, Mindfull, or Mindless

PROCEDURE: Divide your paper into thirds. In the first section, draw a figure or image who appears mindful (e.g., in the present moment, conscious, aware). In the second section, draw a figure or image whose mind is full (e.g., lots of thoughts occurring at one time). In the third section, draw a figure or image who appears mindless (e.g., unaware, thoughtless).

BENEFITS: When you are self-aware of the way you relate to others and approach life, you are able to develop stronger relationships, increase peace and tranquility, reduce stress, and lead a life filled with gratitude and appreciation. Being in touch with your feelings and emotions allows you to take a step back, assess where you are in the moment, and take emotional and physical breaks, especially when your body and mind are telling you to slow down and relax. It allows you to show yourself kindness and true self-compassion, which can help you stay healthier and more energized.

QUESTIONS FOR EXPLORATION:

1. Which of the three categories of mindfulness do you currently relate to the most?

2. What types of figures and symbols did you choose to represent the categories of awareness?

3. Did the way you depict the groupings relate to the way you communicate or approach life?

4. How can focusing on mindfulness transform some of your attitudes and behaviors?

5. Which mindfulness practice would you consider continuing or beginning in the near future (e.g., meditation, yoga, guided imagery, designing mandalas)?

Mini-Intuitive Sculpture

ADDITIONAL MATERIALS: Self-hardening clay, such as Model Magic®.

PROCEDURE: *Group leaders should provide clients with a ball of clay about the size of a small fist and play a soothing musical track for this exercise, such as "Most Relaxing Piano Album in the World Ever" (sold by: The Book Hive, LLC) or "Meditation and Relaxation: Soothing Piano Music with Ocean Waves for Meditation, Focus, Mindfulness, Spa, Yoga & Stress Relief Meditation Music Assembly" (sold on Amazon. com).* Using the ball of clay in front of you, create an unplanned sculpture by just allowing your hands to lead the way as you listen to soft, soothing music. Try to refrain from judging your work. Allow yourself to be spontaneous and see what evolves.

BENEFITS: Participating in this exercise helps you get in touch with your intuition, as opposed to relying on reason or observation. There is no thought process that goes into creating your artwork; rather, it comes from a place that is heart-centered, or what is called the "collective unconscious."[13,14] By tapping into your intuition, you can slow down, relax, quiet your mind, gain clarity, and develop the freedom to be spontaneous.

QUESTIONS FOR EXPLORATION:

1. Were you able to work without planning what you would be creating?

2. Were you able to refrain from judging your work or comparing your work to others?

3. Do you notice any significant meaning or messages conveyed in your competed sculpture?

4. Do you allow yourself to be lighthearted and experiment with creativity in your daily life?

5. Do you allow yourself unstructured time to unwind, be playful, and relax? How does that feel?

6. How can a focus on the creative arts (e.g., music, poetry, art, movement, acting) improve your self-awareness, self-esteem, and motivation?

Upstairs, Downstairs

PROCEDURE: Draw a picture of a two-story house with one door on each story. The door on the second floor represents your future, and the downstairs door represents your past. Next, draw what you might see when you open the doors. Examples may include a relative, an antique piece of furniture, a special possession, emotions (e.g., happiness, sadness, regret), hopes and goals, or something more mysterious or abstract.

BENEFITS: Although living in the present is key, it is sometimes also important to examine your goals, wants, and needs for the future and to make peace with the past. Reconciling your past and present, and looking toward future objectives, can help you feel calmer, more at peace, and more motivated to continue your life journey in a positive manner.

QUESTIONS FOR EXPLORATION:

1. What did you draw behind the doors?

2. What is your reaction to what you placed there?

3. Are you currently focused more on the past, present, or future?

4. How does your focus affect your attitude, mood, and behavior? For example, if you feel stuck in the past, does it increase the likelihood of low self-esteem and depression?

Focusing on Mindfulness

PROCEDURE: Think about the phrase "focus on here, not there." It can be considered an affirmation encouraging you to be in the moment. Fold a piece of paper in half and, on one side of the page, draw what is "here" (e.g., what is in your reality, your environment, or your line of sight right now). On the other side of the page, create an abstract drawing of what is "there" (e.g., the unattainable, the future, or your thoughts about the past).

BENEFITS: This directive reminds you to be mindful and not allow your thoughts to wander too far. What's "here" is concrete and real, whereas what's "there" is generally in the future or past. It's something that is abstract and unattainable. You don't know what the future holds so focusing on what's "there" usually causes frustration, anxiety, and panic.

QUESTIONS FOR EXPLORATION:

1. Which images symbolize what is in your immediate environment and which images symbolize wandering thoughts?

2. How can your mindful affirmation and the associated images you drew help you stay in the here-and-now?

3. Which coping techniques can you use to bring yourself back to "here" when you find yourself "there"?

chapter three

stress & anxiety

Stress and anxiety are a universal aspect of the human condition, as we all experience times of illness, frustration, loss, and interpersonal conflict. However, anxiety can become overwhelming in frequency or degree when you fall into erroneous thinking patterns that perpetuate anxiety, such as catastrophizing (e.g., "This is the end of the world"), overgeneralizing (e.g., "I always mess up"), and labeling (e.g., "I'm a failure"). Part of overcoming anxiety involves identifying and challenging these faulty beliefs, which can be accomplished through thought-stopping, positive self-talk, and identifying realistic and unrealistic fears. Doing so can help you understand the importance that attitude and motivation play in reducing stress, and it can also help you to focus on the positive aspects of your life instead of dwelling on the negative.

You can also reduce stress and anxiety by developing an awareness of your "wise mind." In contrast to "rational mind" and "emotional mind," wise mind involves a deep connection to your intuition. It is a place of intuitive knowing where reason and emotion meet. Importantly, the most effective way to get into wise mind is to practice mindfulness techniques (e.g., deep breathing, focusing on the senses, guided imagery), which can help you find a sense of calm, inner peace, and balance. These practices help you learn how to take it one day at a time, take tiny steps forward, and not allow yourself to be overwhelmed by adversity. In turn, mindfulness can enhance your mood, increase self-confidence, and promote self-acceptance. Some research even shows that mindful meditation may improve immune system functioning, allergies, asthma, cancer, depression, fatigue, heart disease, sleep problems, and high blood pressure.

Additionally, coping with stress and anxiety involves developing an awareness of the harmful roles that you may take on in the context of interpersonal relationships, such as being the victim or scapegoat in the family. You must learn to identify how these negative patterns permeate your relationships and your life, and then try to change or improve them. You can focus on leaning back on your support system and asking for help when needed.

You can also learn how to identify any anxiety triggers and avoid them when possible. You can use self-soothing techniques as a way to mitigate stress, such as creating art, journaling, taking long walks, celebrating achievements, and exercising. Ultimately, you can learn to take care of yourself physically and psychologically, and to focus on your strengths and attributes.

The exercises in this chapter will help clients reduce their anxiety through a variety of art therapy techniques that are intended to promote cognitive restructuring, stress reduction, self-soothing, and mindfulness.

Waves of Change

PROCEDURE: Draw a series of waves and use colors, images, and symbols to describe any changes that you have experienced, changes you are currently experiencing, and possible future changes.

BENEFITS: This exercise helps you become more self-aware of your attitude and behaviors, specifically in terms of how you react to difficulties and changes in your life. Engaging in this exercise helps you strategize and personalize healthy coping skills that you can use to surf the waves of change and keep afloat instead of falling victim to dread, stress, and avoidance.

QUESTIONS FOR EXPLORATION:

1. Are the waves smooth, undulating, or erratic? Are they dark, bright, or multicolored?

2. Do you feel like diving in, swimming cautiously, or avoiding the waves? Is there any fear of falling into the waves?

3. Are the waves new, or have they been there a long time?

4. Are you able to surf the waves, or do you tend to struggle?

5. How do the waves relate to the way you handle change and challenges?

6. Are there any fish, mammals, or other creatures in the waves?

Radiating Peace Outwards

PROCEDURE: Draw a symbol representing anxiety in the center of the paper. Next, create long rays emanating from the anxiety as if they were similar to extended flower petals. The rays should be wide enough to be able to write or draw within them. Each ray should contain images, colors, or shapes that represent a feeling of peace and serenity.

BENEFITS: When you feel anxious, visualize calm, peaceful rays surrounding your anxiety. Try to imagine the calming feelings that each ray evokes with you. Take deep, cleansing breaths and allow yourself to feel the stillness in your body and your surrounding environment. This brief exercise can help lessen stress and discomfort.

QUESTIONS FOR EXPLORATION:

1. How did you represent your anxiety and the rays emerging from it?

2. Is your anxiety manageable, somewhat difficult, or overwhelming?

3. How do the rays promote a feeling of peace and lessen tension?

CLIENT RESPONSE:

A 35-year-old woman named Emily symbolized her anxiety as a horrified figure, copying the style of the artist Edvard Munch. She shared that when she experiences anxiety, she feels like the world is caving in on her and she loses control; sometimes, she hallucinates (e.g., one day she thought she saw her friend walk in the air and stated, "She was well above the ground").

In order to help control her stress, she reported trying to use many coping skills, some of which emanate from the core of her anxiety (as seen in the sketch). They include trying to take deep breaths to stay calm, focusing on herself and not on others, accepting what is happening in her life, and thinking about positive things, like going on vacation, swimming, and bicycle riding. One of the rays in the picture represents the love she has for her family and friends. Emily remarked that the "love ray" is the most significant one, and it is the one that keeps her from incapacitating depression.

Beauty of Butterflies

PROCEDURE: In a realistic or abstract manner, draw or paint a grouping of butterflies. Then, add additional sketches, photos, and images of beauty in the background. *The group leader may choose to distribute outlines of butterflies that can be cut out, filled in with color, and glued on the paper. These outlines may be copied from Google Images® or sketched by the group leader. The images may help certain clients feel more comfortable working on the exercise.*

BENEFITS: Observing butterflies, birds, flowers, flowing streams, green fields, and other serene images tend to help us feel brighter and calmer. A feeling of well-being often replaces negativity when we are viewing the splendor of nature.

QUESTIONS FOR EXPLORATION:

1. In which ways do you find nature soothing?

2. Share one or more beautiful sights you have observed in recent years. How did you feel at that moment in time?

3. What do you see on a daily basis that uplifts your spirit (e.g., colorful gardens, lush foliage, the sunrise, or the sunset)?

4. How can you use nature to become more mindful and peaceful?

Stress Relief
Collage/Sketch Collage

PROCEDURE: Create a grouping of drawings and photos that symbolize ways in which you can decrease anxiety and stress. For example, you could include a photo or sketch of someone exercising, practicing yoga, sitting in a park, journaling, drawing, sewing, knitting, boating, listening to music, petting a dog or cat, etc.

BENEFITS: This exercise helps you develop a repertoire of leisure skills that aid in distraction and anxiety reduction, and that also enhance serenity, focus, and problem solving. You become stronger when you have a variety of relaxation techniques at your fingertips. Problem solving is enhanced as you make decisions regarding ways in which you may relieve stress, and by choosing specific photos to use in your collage.

QUESTIONS FOR EXPLORATION:

1. Which activities seem most doable?

2. Which ones do you currently engage in and which ones do you want to begin in the near future?

3. Which photos attract you the most and seem the most motivating?

Anxiety Tree That Relates to Me

PROCEDURE: Draw an outline of a tree that fills most of the page. *Alternatively, the group leader may provide the outline to group members.* Then, fill in the tree with anything that causes you anxiety or dread, including your problems, worries, concerns, or fears.

BENEFITS: Increasing your awareness of the people, places, and things that create anxiety is the first step toward dealing with anxiety and eventually lessening and perhaps eliminating it. When you draw or write about your stress, you are better able to distance yourself from it and gain more control. It allows you the opportunity to analyze your worries and develop coping techniques to deal with them. You don't "own" your anxiety as intensely when you bring it out in the open for exploration.

QUESTIONS FOR EXPLORATION:

1. What type of tree did you draw? Think about its size, shape, and color.

2. Is your tree full or sparse? Does it seem to be thriving or does it appear stagnant?

3. What have you placed on your tree? What is your reaction to the concerns included?

4. Are your fears or worries realistic?

5. Are your worries within your control?

6. Are the things you fear imminent?

7. How likely are the things you worry about going to happen?

8. Is there any other way of viewing your concerns?

9. How can you channel your worry so you can feel calmer and become more productive?

10. How does worrying help you? How does it harm you?

11. Will you allow yourself to "let go" of your worries for at least a little while? Perhaps you can give yourself a vacation from your worries.

12. Is there something you can do right now that is more productive than worrying and feeling stressed? What can serve as a distraction?

CLIENT RESPONSE:

Joe, a 41-year-old man who often worked as an extra in Hollywood movies, drew a fragile, "scrawny," tree with a shaky base. He stated that the tree could fall down at any moment and that the ground it was planted upon was muddy, unstable, and cracked. He added a variety of holes in the tree to represent traumas in his life, such as his parents' divorce at age 8 and a car accident at age 16 where he was thrown from the car and broke both arms, a leg, and a number of ribs, but miraculously survived. His best friend died in the accident.

Tongue in cheek, Joe remarked that his depression is strong, but his tree is "a weak mess." He related his current depression to an impending divorce, financial problems, and severe migraines that seemed never-ending. He did say that he was trying to practice coping skills, such as deep breathing and meditation. He shared that he enjoyed art and stated it helped him express his feelings and feel more relaxed.

Uncoiling Anxiety I

PROCEDURE: Draw yourself unwinding. Envision yourself as a spiral or helix disentangling. Think of a coil, and imagine it knotted up at first and slowly untwisting in order to be less compressed. You may attempt to do this exercise in a realistic or abstract manner.

BENEFITS: Designing, observing, and examining your personal coil, and then creatively unwinding it, is a first step toward understanding your emotions, what creates stress in your life, and what tools you need to begin to reduce anxiety and stress. The exercise serves as a reminder to take mental health breaks and increase awareness of "who, what, and when" adds anxiety to your daily routine.

QUESTIONS FOR EXPLORATION:

1. What did your coil look like at first, and how does it appear when less tightly knotted?

2. How can you relate to the coil?

3. What do you do to unwind? What would you like to do in the future to reduce stress?

75

CLIENT RESPONSE:

A 64-year-old woman named Marietta drew herself as a flower unwinding bit by bit. She shared that her stress starts as a seed (bottom left of the flower), which is very small, but tight and compressed. The seed starts to grow and becomes less compressed, but still remains knotted and uncomfortably tight. This is the point where Marietta feels confused and distraught, which is usually brought upon by work and relationship problems.

Marietta stated that her anxiety continues for some time but eventually begins to uncoil little by little until it stretches out and a flower blooms. This is when she feels calmer and more at peace. It is during those times that life is "good for her." According to Marietta, the flower represents how something positive can come from negativity if you have patience. Marietta also added that her serenity is usually short-lived and that the ground, which she characterized as dark and dangerous like quicksand, could "swallow up the flower at any time."

Uncoiling Anxiety II

PROCEDURE: Represent your anxiety as a coil. On the same page, or on another sheet of paper, begin to unwind the coil slowly by drawing it untwisting bit by bit. You may do this in any unique way you please, or by drawing a long wavy line that appears to have been disentangled. On each wave or part of the coil, write or draw a symbol of ways to reduce anxiety, including grounding techniques. Examples may include deep breathing, meditation, filling in adult coloring outlines, guided imagery, or focusing on your senses.

BENEFITS: By visualizing your anxiety physically uncoiling itself, you can stop or limit the spiraling of anxiety and hopefully avoid a full-blown anxiety attack. It allows you to gain control of your thoughts and feelings and focus on being in the moment instead, which can help lower blood pressure and slow heart rate.

QUESTIONS FOR EXPLORATION:

1. How would you describe the appearance of your anxiety coil and the unraveling coil?

2. What techniques are represented on the unraveling coil?

3. How long is the unraveling coil, and how effective do you think the methods included will be for you in times of need?

Anxiety as an Appendage

PROCEDURE: Imagine your anxiety is like an appendage that is attached to your body with Velcro®. It can be a ball-like growth, an extra hand, a squiggle, or whatever shape you want to imagine. Now, draw a human figure with this appendage attached to it, or just draw the appendage itself. As you draw, think about its size, shape, form, and color. *The group leader can also provide an outline of the human form to those who desire more structure.*

BENEFITS: This visualization exercise allows you to explore what triggers your stress and helps you develop methods to diminish its impact on your life. Envisioning stress helps you distance yourself from it, understand it, and better control it. The stress loses some of its grip on your thinking, attitude, and functioning.

QUESTIONS FOR EXPLORATION:

1. What type of appendage did you design?

2. How much of your body does it cover?

3. How strongly attached is it?

4. How long has it been there?

5. How does it affect your mood, motivation, relationships, and general behavior?

6. Are you ready to detach it?

7. Do you need assistance to detach it?

8. How would you feel if you did remove it?

Wandering of My Anxiety

PROCEDURE: Draw the way anxious thoughts wander through your mind. Think about how and where they begin, the way they travel, and where they end up. For example, do they meander gently through your mind? Do they increase and decrease sharply? Do they zigzag? Do they tend to spiral out of control? Do they erupt like a volcano? Do they form knots, or do they stay in one place, becoming increasingly tight and pressured? In addition, are there specific feelings and images associated with your anxious thoughts?

BENEFITS: Engaging in this exercise helps you acquire new perspectives regarding what elicits anxiety and how stress affects your disposition, emotions, and behavior. When you have an increased awareness of how anxiety evolves, you are better able to recognize and understand it.

QUESTIONS FOR EXPLORATION:

1. What does your anxiety look like?

2. What feelings are elicited when you observe your anxiety art?

3. Are you able to relate your drawing to the way your anxiety generally moves throughout your body and mind?

4. Do you notice any points on the page where your anxiety slowed down or became more intense?

5. What would you like to say to your anxiety? For example, you might want to say, "Calm down," "Leave me alone," or "You don't control me."

Stretched and Drawn-Out

PROCEDURE: Create a sketch that answers the question, "How are you being stretched in your life?" Think about obligations, family, work, thoughts, worries, etc. You may draw what is stretching you specifically, or a figure symbolizing you actually being stretched.

BENEFITS: In today's fast-paced society, we sometimes become entrenched in and numb to our routines, which can create stress and anxiety, and even lead to failing physical health. This exercise helps you take a step back and notice how you are living your life. It allows you to explore your daily patterns and ask yourself if you are allowing time to rest and heal. If your life is too frenzied, then you may benefit by changing parts of your routine and obligations so you can feel stronger, healthier, and more in control.

QUESTIONS FOR EXPLORATION:

1. How stretched is your figure?

2. Are your limits stretched now?

3. If your figure is overly stretched, are there ways you can tweak some of your obligations and duties?

4. How do your responsibilities affect your mood, emotions, and motivation?

5. If your figure is too overstretched, would you like to change the way the figure is drawn? Would you like to create another figure that is less drawn-out? How might doing that symbolically be of help?

CLIENT RESPONSE:

Kevin, a 28-year-old man with a variety of problems, including addiction, drew his center as a distressed light bulb. Kevin mentioned that he feels like his head isn't screwed on right, noting that "sometimes it is too tight, and sometimes it is too loose." He shared that he is being stretched in ways that are distracting and stressful. Kevin remarked that he wants to go back to college to study music (guitar in the upper right) but feels too anxious; he said he can't concentrate for more than a few minutes. Kevin complained that he owes his parents and others too much money and felt weighed down by bricks (bottom left), bills, and obligations.

He stated that his only hope, represented by the small window above the bulb, is that there is some light at the end of the tunnel. He was hoping that his medication, which had recently been changed, would make him feel calmer and more focused so he would be able to better cope with all his responsibilities. He shared that if he had more energy and wasn't so nervous, then he could at least begin to explore ways to work on his issues and goals.

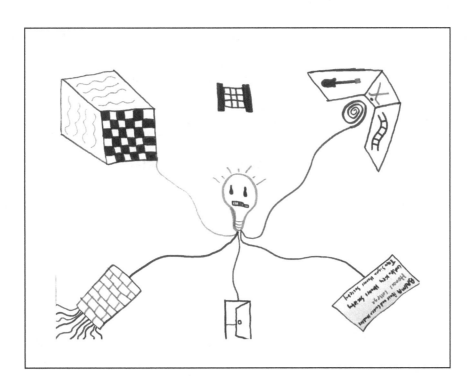

Worry Box to Store Troubles

PROCEDURE: Decorate a small white or light brown box with personal designs, small shapes, doodles, positive words, and affirmations. Next, write a few worries or concerns on small strips of paper and place the papers in the box. Then, store the box in a place that is out of sight. When you feel worried of stressed, write or sketch the worry on a small strip of paper and place it in the box. Once a week, or whenever you feel the need, review the contents of the box and decide if you want to keep certain worries or throw some of them out (e.g., let them go). You may then dispose of the strips of paper by throwing them in the garbage or ripping them up. Your mood and the intensity of the concern may dictate how you dispose of them.

BENEFITS: Designing this personal box, and keeping it hidden but handy for future exploration, will enable you to gain better control of your anxiety. Stress is lessened by separating yourself from your concerns and gaining control over them by deciding whether or not they are worth keeping.

QUESTIONS FOR EXPLORATION:

1. Does the outside of the box reflect your mood, stress level, or personality?

2. Did you decorate the box with affirmations that you find particularly useful?

3. Is your box currently full, partially full, or empty?

4. Are there any concerns you are ready to let go of today?

5. How can a stress box help you reduce anxiety and separate yourself from worries for at least a while?

"Here to There" Design

PROCEDURE: Create a drawing that depicts where you are now and where you want to be. As you create your drawing, think about your environment, home, work situation, relationships, health, financial status, etc.

BENEFITS: Working on this exercise enhances self-awareness by allowing you to explore future goals and ways to achieve them. Possible frustrations about present circumstances may be identified, examined, and worked upon to increase motivation and improve life satisfaction.

QUESTIONS FOR EXPLORATION:

1. How do you feel about your current situation?

2. How much of a discrepancy is there between where you are now and where you'd like to be?

3. Does this discrepancy affect your mood, thoughts, motivation, self-worth, or behavior?

4. How did you symbolize this discrepancy in your artwork?

5. Which part of your artwork did you spend the most time creating, or did you give equal attention to the "here" and "there"?

6. Are your goals (the "there") attainable? Are they realistic?

7. Do you have a plan to reach your goals?

> "Stress is caused by being 'here'
> but wanting to be 'there.'"
>
> – Eckhart Tolle

Pushing Away Anxiety

PROCEDURE: Draw yourself pushing away anxiety and unpleasant emotions. You may represent this theme realistically or abstractly, using line, shape and color. An example may include a figure with large hands pushing his anxious thoughts (e.g., red spirals) into a wall.

BENEFITS: You learn to deal with anxiety by exploring its origins, meaning, triggers, and intensity. Through this drawing, you are able to better analyze, understand, and control your anxiety as you symbolically push it away.

QUESTIONS FOR EXPLORATION:

1. What is the size and strength of the figure in relation to the anxiety?

2. Does the figure or the anxiety seem to be in control, or is it about equal?

3. Is the figure actively or passively dealing with the anxiety?

4. In which ways do you relate to this depiction?

5. What would you like to say to the figure or the anxiety?

Fist Filled with Frustration

PROCEDURE: Draw a closed or clenched fist in a realistic or abstract manner, and decorate it with people, places, thoughts, and things you find frustrating.[1] Next, draw an open hand (you may do this by tracing the outline of your hand), and fill it in with ways to relieve the frustration you are experiencing. For example, you can focus on your strengths and abilities, practice acceptance, volunteer to help others, or distract yourself with hobbies and interests, such as listening to music, creating art, or playing with a pet.

BENEFITS: Your hands are amazing structures that allow you to do a huge amount of helpful and wonderful things every day. They are helping you engage in this art therapy exercise right now. Your hands can also inform you of your current emotional state. When you are relaxed, your hands are often opened in a stress-free position, but when you feel anxious, a fist often forms. A clenched fist can mean many things, such as anger, annoyance, fear, stress, or frustration. It can also mean that you are feeling short-tempered, have the urge to fight, or are hiding something. This fixed position can be harmful if it occurs too often. Self-awareness is the first step toward relaxing your fist, coping with your frustrations, and taking some of the burden off your body and soul. By developing this self-awareness, you can express your feelings and frustrations, actively explore ways to cope and work through them, and finally accept your current circumstances.

QUESTIONS FOR EXPLORATION:

1. How did you feel while you designed the fist, and how did you feel while you designed the opened hand?

2. What did you include in the fist and in the opened hand?

3. Today are you more drawn to the fist or the opened hand?

4. In what ways does the "fist" help you and in what ways does it hurt you?

5. How does a focus on the opened hand aid in relaxation and motivation to move on?

6. Are you able to tolerate living, at least temporarily, with both the fist and the opened hand?

Toleration Pie

PROCEDURE: Create a pie by using a paper plate to form the outline of a circle, and then fill it in with ways to tolerate stressful situations. You may decorate the pie in a variety of ways, including dividing it into slices of coping skills, such a deep breathing, sketching, and meditation. Six to eight slices is optimal. You may also add toppings, such as chocolate chips and sprinkles, while thinking about the pie's benefits.

BENEFITS: Tolerating stress helps you function and cope with everyday life. It enables you to view situations from more than one angle, and it helps your body relax and work effectively. It keeps you from staying stuck in the mud. This exercise can remind you to ask yourself, "Is there any part of this situation I can possibly tolerate?" the next time you are in an anxiety-provoking situation. Even if you can accept some small part of the situation, healing begins.

QUESTIONS FOR EXPLORATION:

1. What type of pie did you create, and how effective do you think it will be in reducing stress?

2. Which slice do you think will be most effective?

3. Is there anyone you would like to share a slice of the pie with in order to help them feel stronger?

4. How long do you think the pie will last? Will you remember what it tasted like (the coping skills listed) after it has been consumed?

Coping When Unfairly Treated

PROCEDURE: Draw a person, animal, or imaginary creature in the center of a 8.5 × 11 inch or larger sheet of paper. Next, create an environment around it that appears ominous, such as lightning strikes, clouds, a dark gray rainy sky, or fiery shapes. On another sheet of paper, draw a positive image or shape, such as a sunrise, or write a positive word or phrase, such as, "I am strong." You can also use magazine photos for this exercise. Then, cut out the positive shape, word, or phrase, and tape or glue it somewhere on the original drawing to provide symbolic relief to the person, animal, or creature situated in the middle of the page.

BENEFITS: Working on this exercise helps you develop coping skills to handle the occasional unfairness of life and bullying from others, such as a strict boss, unfair teacher, domineering partner, angry friend or neighbor, or critical family member. It also reminds you to practice self-soothing strategies when you feel wrongfully criticized or punished.

QUESTIONS FOR EXPLORATION:

1. What type of figure and environment did you depict?

2. Is the environment frightening or menacing? If so, to what degree?

3. How does the figure appear in relation to the environment? For example, is the figure tiny or cowering, or does the figure seem to stand up to the hazards surrounding it?

4. Do you relate more to the figure or the environment?

5. How can you cope when you are in psychological pain or being treated unfairly?

6. In what ways can you self-soothe when you feel stressed and vulnerable?

Illogical Mode

PROCEDURE: Draw what your mind looks like when it is in illogical mode. Think about the organization, patterns, shapes, colors, connections, and disconnections that characterize your mind in this mode. Examples of illogical thinking include the fear that everyone dislikes you or that your family would be better off if you moved far away.

BENEFITS: When you become aware of illogical thinking, you are able to utilize coping skills, such as sensory awareness and deep breathing, in order to think more rationally. You become more reality-oriented, gain better self-control, and feel less disconnected and fearful.

QUESTIONS FOR EXPLORATION:

1. What happens to your brain in illogical mode? What do you notice about the activity that takes place in your brain during this period of time as it relates to your artwork?

2. Are there specific triggers that may create irrational thinking or behavior?

3. Which coping skills do you think may help?

4. How would self-awareness of unhealthy thinking patterns help you make healthier choices when you feel very stressed and are beginning to spiral out of control?

CLIENT RESPONSE:

Adam, a 36-year-old man with addiction issues and PTSD, drew Fort Knox. He stated that when he is in illogical mode, his mind often tells him that people in his life think he is worthless. He stated that he believes they tease him about his low-paying job and his appearance. For example, he shared that he thinks his wife and parents make fun of his slightly crossed eyes and bright red hair. Adam remarked that on one level, he knows his family loves him, but when he is in "crazy mode," he becomes very paranoid. Fort Knox, which he designed using bricks and a moat with alligators in front of it, is his defense. He stated that he attempts to keep himself safe from upsetting feelings by going to sleep so he doesn't have to experience these uncomfortable feelings. He shared that sleep (his Fort Knox) keeps him from focusing on his stress and possibly becoming suicidal.

Filling My Worry Cloud

PROCEDURE: Draw a large cloud covering most of the paper, and fill it in with drawings, images, symbols, or magazine photos that symbolize your concerns, fears, and worries.[2]

BENEFITS: Engaging in this exercise allows you to externalize your worries and concerns. By distancing yourself from your anxiety, you can more effectively problem solve how to deal with it and facilitate positive change.

QUESTIONS FOR EXPLORATION:

1. How full is your cloud? Is it being weighed down or is it light and airy?

2. Which worries fill up most of the cloud?

3. Have your concerns been in the cloud for a long time, or have they been recently added to the cloud?

4. Would you characterize your cloud as changeable or stagnant?

5. How has your cloud changed over the years?

Rooted to the Ground

PROCEDURE: Draw a realistic or abstract figure with roots attached that are spreading into the ground beneath it. These roots represent that which makes you feel grounded and secure.

BENEFITS: Grounding techniques reduce anxiety and may ward off an anxiety attack. One of many helpful grounding techniques includes imagining that you are rooted to the ground like a tree. Viewing yourself in this way may help you feel more stable, strong, and reality-oriented when you enter illogical or anxious mind. Other grounding techniques include placing ice cubes on your neck and wrists, focusing on your senses, and eating something very spicy, cold, or hot.

QUESTIONS FOR EXPLORATION:

1. How is the figure drawn? Is it large or small, sturdy or fragile, colorful or dull?

2. Are the roots deep and complex, or weak and shallow?

3. How does the figure and its root system relate to your own stability and relationship to your environment?

4. Would you consider using this technique when you are feeling extremely anxious?

CLIENT RESPONSE:

A 28-year-old woman named Iris drew her ankles almost strangled with roots that led beneath the dark brown earth. She shared she felt trapped, not rooted. She remarked that, sometimes, she feels so anxious and apprehensive about almost all of the things she has to do on a daily basis, including grocery shopping, that she can hardly move. Iris remarked that she was working on self-compassion, not worrying what others thought of her, and trying to take baby steps to move forward.

Treasure Chest of Coping Thoughts

PROCEDURE: Draw an elaborate treasure chest and fill it with thoughts, phrases, and affirmations that are calming, introspective, and uplifting. You may design symbols to represent the thoughts and/or write them using markers or gel pens. You can also use magazine photos. Some examples of coping statements include:

- "This is temporary."

- "This too shall pass."

- "My feelings make me feel uncomfortable right now, but I can accept them."

- "I can ride this out and not let it get to me."

- "My anxiety won't kill me; it just doesn't feel good right now."

- "I will not allow my feelings to control me."

- "It's okay to make mistakes."

- "I've survived other situations like this before, and I'll survive this one too."

- "I am enough."

- "I'm strong and I can deal with this."

- "So what?"

- "I can't change others, but I can change my reaction to them."

BENEFITS: Creating a treasure chest of helpful thoughts and affirmations can motivate you and provide a sense of relief, acceptance, and self-worth in times of stress. They can inspire you to accept yourself as you are and allow yourself to experiment, make mistakes, and learn and grow at your own pace. You can realize that you are only human and are doing your best in what is sometimes a turbulent world.

QUESTIONS FOR EXPLORATION:

1. How does your treasure chest symbolize the amount of positivity in your life now? Is it large enough to contain all of your encouraging thoughts and affirmations?

2. Which affirmations or uplifting thoughts are your favorites? In what ways do they inspire you?

3. Which affirmations have you been using to help you deal with problems and/ or anxiety?

4. Are you deserving of this decorative chest?

5. How often will you utilize it? Will it be a useful addition to your repertoire of coping skills?

Body Exit for Anxiety

PROCEDURE: Draw the outline of a person that covers most of the page. *The group leader can also distribute an outline of the human form to those who desire more structure.* Fill in the areas that represent where you generally feel the most anxiety (e.g., a red circle in the chest or head area). Next, envision one or more routes that the anxiety might take to leave your body, and represent this exit route using lines, colors, and shape (e.g., a light blue wavy line leaving your stomach, moving past your chest, up through your shoulder, down your arm into your hand, and then finally moving out through your fingertips).[3]

BENEFITS: Participating in this exercise will help you better understand and control your anxiety. Greater awareness of anxiety symptoms within your body and the effect anxiety has on your physical and emotional state helps lessen it. Visually and creatively allowing anxiety to exit your body can be generalized toward practical use. This may entail practicing your own unique guided imagery that mimics your "Body Exit" artwork.

QUESTIONS FOR EXPLORATION:

1. Where in your body do you usually feel most of your anxiety?
2. How did you portray the exit route(s) that anxiety takes to leave your body?
3. What colors, designs, and shapes did you use to symbolize this departure?
4. Are you also able to visualize this scenario when you relax and close your eyes?

Stress Reduction Mandala

PROCEDURE: Using a paper plate, make an outline of a circle to form a mandala, and fill it in with ways to reduce stress. You may use words and phrases, or you can use images, designs, and magazine photos.

BENEFITS: This mandala art technique enhances mindfulness and soothes the mind as you explore techniques to help you reduce anxiety and increase control of illogical and/or chaotic thinking.

QUESTIONS FOR EXPLORATION:

1. Which techniques seem most helpful?
2. Which ones will you begin to employ today or this week?
3. Which ideas are very new to you and which ones have you used in the past?
4. How does creatively placing the coping skills within the mandala assist you to examine and explore them?

Invaders Among Us

PROCEDURE: Invaders are those stressful, negative thoughts that adversely affect your self-esteem and motivation. Using a piece of paper, draw your invaders. What do they look like? Think about their size, shape, movement, impact, and intensity.

BENEFITS: In order to lessen or eliminate your invaders, you first need to be cognizant of their existence. By placing your invaders on paper and giving them a form or identity, you can gain some sense of control over them. It gives you an opportunity to distance yourself from them while better understanding the impact they have on your mood and behavior.

QUESTIONS FOR EXPLORATION:

1. What type of invaders did you draw? Do they appear ominous, strong, weak, silly, or cartoon-like?

2. Are there many invaders or just a few? How often do they seem to pop up?

3. Are there personal or environmental triggers that help them multiply?

4. Where do you think the invaders came from? For example, did they arise from your parents, friends, school, work, or unfortunate experiences?

5. Are you in the process of developing plans to deal with them? Is there a coping skill you find effective now?

CLIENT RESPONSE:

Rita, a 56-year-old mother of three adult children, laughed aloud after she drew this picture. She remarked that she had fun drawing and just sketched whatever came to mind. She liked the little creatures she designed and thought they certainly captured some of her stressful feelings. When she further examined her work, she realized that there were three creatures and, ironically, that she had three children. Rita stated her children do cause her stress, each one for a different reason. She remarked that she might need a vacation from her children's issues, which could be overwhelming at times. One of her children was going through a divorce and another was experiencing addiction issues.

Observing My Anxiety

PROCEDURE: Draw your anxiety as if you were observing it from afar, much like being in the audience of a movie or play. Think about its size, shape, and appearance. Consider the way it affects your mood, as well as the way it interacts with the environment.

BENEFITS: Observing your anxiety from a distance allows you to detach yourself from it so you can better analyze it, view it from a different perspective, and get a better handle on it. In doing so, the anxiety no longer feels as consuming; you don't "own" it as much. Instead, you gain increased control over it, which makes you stronger and increases your motivation and self-worth.

QUESTIONS FOR EXPLORATION:

1. What is your assessment of your anxiety?

2. How does it appear? For example, is it large or small? Sharp or soft? Threatening or inconsequential?

3. Is anxiety prevalent in your life? How long have you experienced it?

4. How can being mindful help you better deal with anxiety and stress?

Yesterday, Today, Tomorrow

PROCEDURE: Before beginning this activity, read the following quote:

> "Yesterday is history,
> Tomorrow is a mystery.
> Today is a gift,
> That's why they call it the present."

Then, take a piece of a paper and fold it into thirds. In the first section, draw something that is representative of yesterday (e.g., your past). In the second section, draw something that reflects where you are today (e.g., the present – your gift). Finally, in the third section, draw something that signifies tomorrow (e.g., your future – a mystery).

BENEFITS: Reviewing your history can be a useful reminder of past achievements and obstacles that you have overcome. Similarly, glancing at the future may be helpful for planning potential goals and seeking opportunities. The idea is not to dwell on the past or future, as you can't change the past and the future is not guaranteed. Dwelling on the remnants of yesterday or the uncertainty of tomorrow will only cause anxiety. Rather, reviewing the gifts that you bring today can help you stay in the here-and-now and feel calmer and in more control.

QUESTIONS FOR EXPLORATION:

1. What did you draw to represent the present, and what is the significance of the drawing?

2. Which section did you fill in first, and which section was easiest versus most difficult to fill in?

3. What techniques do you employ to stay in the here-and-now?

4. What are the benefits of mindfulness?

Talking Back to Anxiety

PROCEDURE: Draw yourself talking back to your anxiety. You may represent yourself and your anxiety in any creative manner you please. For example, your anxiety may be portrayed as a monster, animal, person, insect, amorphous shape, or creature. You can refute your anxiety by saying:

- "I don't have to think this way."

- "I am stronger than you."

- "I will not be a victim."

- "I am safe."

- "I will focus on my breath."

- "This too shall pass."

- "I can distract myself to feel better."

- "I can ride this out."

- "I will not allow you to control me."

- "I will focus on my senses and send you away."

- "Today I will call someone for support to help stop you."

BENEFITS: By talking back to your anxiety, you begin to gain control over it and the anxiety starts to become less overwhelming. When you don't remain in the victim role, your anxiety no longer seems as scary.

QUESTIONS FOR EXPLORATION:

1. How did you portray yourself and your anxiety?

2. Which figure appears dominant?

3. What are you saying to your anxiety?

4. What techniques do you use to deal with stress?

5. What techniques would you like to implement now or in the future?

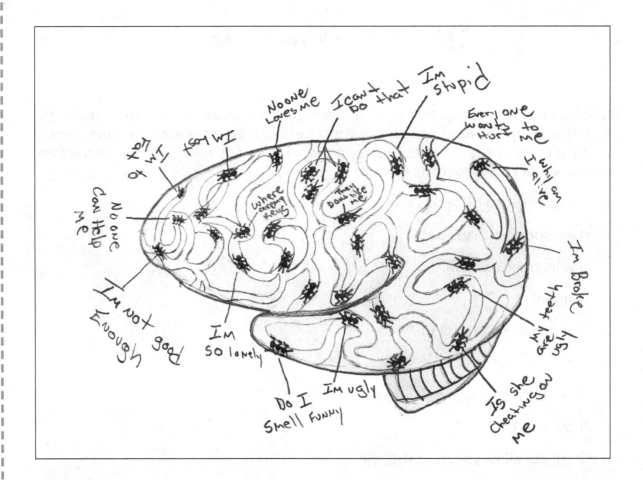

CLIENT RESPONSE:

Derek, a 39-year-old man with bipolar disorder and addiction issues, drew a brain filled with an abundance of ants, which represent negative thinking. He stated, "The ants are all over my brain, in every nook and crevice." The following are some of the cognitive distortions that the ants represented: *"I'm so lonely," "No one will ever date me," "I'm not good enough,"* and *"Do I smell funny?"* Derek shared that this was the first time he realized how his negative thinking patterns impacted his relationships. He remarked that he understood that his negativity was probably a major reason for his lack of friends and low-level job. His goal was to fight the ants using his brain; he characterized himself as smart academically, and he did see that as a valuable asset.

Stress Stone

PROCEDURE: Draw a large stone on a piece of paper and fill it in with symbols and words that represent your current stressors. While you are drawing, try to place the stone near a body of water like a lake, river, or stream.[4] After the drawing is complete, think about the stone and decide if you want to rid yourself of your stress. If so, imagine throwing the stone in the water. Think about the way it falls into the water, try to hear the splash, and through your mind's eye watch it sink slowly downward toward the bottom of the lake, river, or stream.

BENEFITS: This exercise allows you to take control of stress as you visualize all your worries, concerns, and fears sinking to the bottom of a body of water. Using visual imagery and distraction techniques such as this allows you to free yourself from stress, even if just for a little while.

QUESTIONS FOR EXPLORATION:

1. What size is your stone? What did you draw or write on it?

2. How does it look? Is it full of stress or nearly stress-free? Is it dark or bright? Dull or shiny? Full of color? Black, gray, brown?

3. How long have you had your stone? Has it grown in size recently?

4. What do you want to do with the stone today? Would throwing it away right now help you?

5. Do you ever take a break from stress?

Anxiety Break

PROCEDURE: Draw what an anxiety break would look like for you. For example, it could involve taking a walk in the park, engaging in a brief mediation, doing a few minutes of yoga, sipping a cup of tea, petting your dog, focusing on your breathing, eating frozen yogurt while enjoying the sun, or turning off all technology.

BENEFITS: Taking a break from anxiety and engaging in self-care is important in reducing stress and promoting self-compassion. Sometimes, you have to practice being kind to yourself and give yourself permission to take mental health breaks throughout the day. These brief pauses help you relax, reboot, and energize.

QUESTIONS FOR EXPLORATION:

1. How does your artwork reflect your current needs and goals relating to self-care?

2. What do the images in your art convey to you about time management?

3. Is someone or something blocking you from taking anxiety breaks during the day, or do you have a period where you can relax and unwind?

4. Do you allow yourself to take "time outs" during the day?

5. How would taking anxiety breaks help you function more effectively?

Mind Over Matter

PROCEDURE: Take a piece of 8½ × 11 inch paper and fold it into thirds vertically, and then in half horizontally, so that there are six total boxes on the page. Next, draw an outline of a brain in each of the three **bottom** rectangles. *Alternatively, the group leader can distribute templates of a brain for participants to outline.* Inside each of the three brain outlines, draw or write one problem or concern.

Next, within each rectangle on the **top** row, draw at least one way to work through the issue that is represented in the brain directly underneath it. For example, if one of the brains in the bottom row contains an anxiety symbol, then the picture drawn above it may represent someone practicing yoga or meditating.

BENEFITS: This exercise helps you problem solve and learn to connect specific coping skills with specific issues and stressors. It helps you put mind over matter as you focus on what you can do to overcome what's in your way instead of allowing negative self-talk to influence you. As you add new insights and techniques to your coping skills toolbox, you become stronger and better able to deal with adverse situations. You become enlightened and empowered as you continue to understand the tremendous impact that your thinking plays in your attitude, mood, choices, and behavior.

QUESTIONS FOR EXPLORATION:

1. In which ways does your artwork represent your most pertinent concerns?

2. Do you see how balancing worries with a positive mindset can increase emotional and physical health?

3. What are your typical thinking patterns?

4. Of the three concerns depicted in your artwork, which one are you ready to start working through with your identified plan?

> "Where there's a will there's a way."

Blowing Away Stress

PROCEDURE: Draw a large face or profile of a person blowing feathers out of their mouth. The feathers symbolize all of your stress, worry, and intrusive thoughts. You might choose to write your worries on the feathers themselves, or use other images, shapes, and colors to represent your stressors.[5]

BENEFITS: This creative, mindful technique allows you to lessen your worries as you visualize yourself blowing away intrusive thoughts like feathers.

QUESTIONS FOR EXPLORATION:

1. How many feathers are being blown away?

2. Are any of the feathers more difficult to eliminate than others?

3. What type of feathers did you draw? Are they large or small? Colorful or dull? Oddly shaped or more traditional in nature?

4. How does it feel to blow away anxiety? Is this visualization something you might use in the future to help calm your mind?

Chains of Anxiety

PROCEDURE: Draw a grouping of chains varying in size and shape while thinking about things in your life that are holding you back from peace and serenity. *The group leader may distribute copies or outlines of chains for reference.*

BENEFITS: The first step toward loosening or breaking the chains of anxiety is to become aware that they exist, including how and when they developed. By completing this exercise, you can explore the strength of your chains, their importance, and your role if the chains appear indestructible. For example, are you keeping the chains in place because you are fearful or uncomfortable with change? Sometimes, we are afraid of breaking the chains even though the freedom would be healthy for us emotionally and physically.

QUESTIONS FOR EXPLORATION:

1. How would you describe the drawing? Is it full of chains or are they scattered? Are the chains ominous looking or do they appear frail?

2. How are you chained in life? Are you chained to a person, idea, job, or relationship?

3. Which chains keep you chained to stress and negativity?

4. Are you able to function with the chains or do they immobilize you?

5. Do the chains interfere with your functioning? Do they affect your mood?

6. How long have the chains been connected to you? How did they become attached to you?

7. What would life be like with fewer chains or without chains?

8. Do the chains help you in any way?

9. Do you have a plan of action to weaken the chains?

Mapping Out Change

PROCEDURE: The following directive is adapted from Deah Schwartz:[6]

Write a list or think about changes that will be occurring in the near or distant future. Color-code these changes in terms of difficulty, with red being those that are most challenging or stressful, and blue being those that are a little easier to manage or less worrisome. With this color code system in mind, draw a road map similar to a "road itinerary," with each life change representing a stopping point along the way. Using images or symbols, draw what roadside assistance services can help you manage these changes. For example, on a road trip it is important to know where you can get gas or meals along the way, or where to find a rest stop or a place for scenic viewing. On your personal map, a healthful stop may include a park to practice deep breathing or meditation, or a restaurant to self-soothe with hot chocolate or a cup of your favorite coffee or tea.

BENEFITS: This exercise helps you view the changes that lie ahead and instills a sense of control over your future circumstances. Although change is sometimes exciting and long-awaited, the prospect of change can be difficult and anxiety-provoking when too many changes occur at once. By creating a map of the changes that lie ahead in your life, you can reduce stress and find effective ways to manage the anxiety associated with these changes.

QUESTIONS FOR EXPLORATION:

1. Which changes are outlined on your map?

2. How would you describe the road ahead?

3. Are there safety measures and comfort stops included? How might the comfort stops help?

4. Is your map detailed and controlled, or is it disorganized?

5. How can you make future changes less stressful?

6. In general, how do you react to life's changes?

106

Problem/Solution

PROCEDURE: Draw an outline of a head on a sheet of paper and divide it in half. On one half of the head, symbolize a problem you are having using lines, shapes, images, and color. On the other side of the head, symbolize a solution to this problem. For example, on one side of a woman's face, there might be tears and small sketches of children to represent being an empty nester (e.g., her problem). On the other side, there might be the hint of a smile and a woman in a yoga pose to symbolize acceptance and finding new activities to keep her busy and satisfied (e.g., her solution).

BENEFITS: Engaging in this exercise allows you to problem solve and examine "what works." By exploring possible solutions to something that is causing you stress or anxiety, you gain back control and enhance your ability to think abstractly.

QUESTIONS FOR EXPLORATION:

1. Which side of the head was your main focus?

2. Did you arrive at a solution for your problem, or are you still in process?

3. How intense would you rate the problem on a ten-point scale, where one is the least extreme and ten is the most extreme?

4. Were you able to put your issue into perspective? Were you able to brainstorm possible solutions that would be beneficial?

Evil Doppelgänger

PROCEDURE: Divide your page in half, and draw a picture of your evil doppelgänger (e.g., evil twin) on one side of the page. Your evil doppelgänger is the part of you that may appear when you are in emotional mind (e.g., when you are having a panic attack, thinking illogically, acting impulsively, or lashing out in anger). On the other side of the page, draw another sketch to challenge the doppelgänger, such as a peaceful scene or calming thoughts.[7]

BENEFITS: This exercise gives you an opportunity to confront the part of you that is sometimes disorganized, confused, and engages in destructive ways of thinking and behaving. Focusing on the doppelgänger helps you become increasingly aware of the part of your personality that may need more loving care, structure, and a watchful eye. It allows you to examine which coping techniques you can use to tame this evil twin.

QUESTIONS FOR EXPLORATION:

1. How would you describe your doppelgänger? Is it large or small? Frightening or benign?

2. Which are the most effective ways you have to challenge it? Are there other techniques you are contemplating?

3. When did your doppelgänger emerge? What were the precipitating factors?

4. When is it likely to appear? For example, when you are very stressed or when you visit a particular person?

5. When was the last time you had to deal with your doppelgänger? Was your defense effective?

CLIENT RESPONSE:

Artie, a 59-year-old biologist, drew the "Good One," as a professional person who takes his work seriously, and his evil twin "as a lazy, drug addict bum who doesn't care about anything. He is smoking and drinking, throwing garbage on the floor and is overweight." Artie's doppelgänger is sloppy, has long, unwashed hair, and is selfish and uncaring toward others. He still has the brain of a teenager. Artie shared that he struggles between the two personalities, and, unfortunately, the evil twin often takes over his body and mind. Artie has been struggling for years with alcohol addiction and bipolar disorder. He has managed to keep his job, and his family still adores him, even though he has been a problem much of the time. He shared that he is very lucky that his family deals with his quirks and his weaknesses, and they accept him unconditionally.

Lifelines for Coping with Stress

PROCEDURE: Draw your main stressors in the center of the page and then design lifelines emanating from the stressors that you can use to help mitigate a panic attack. These lifelines can represent coping skills you can use (e.g., deep breathing, mindfulness, guided imagery) to get you through a difficult situation, or people or places you can turn to for support. The stressors can be drawn in a realistic or abstract manner.

BENEFITS: Engaging in this exercise helps you identify and solidify at least a few strategies you can use to cope with stress and anxiety. Increasing awareness of lifelines and calling upon them in times of stress is an important tool for tolerating difficult situations, especially when you are very anxious or depressed.

QUESTIONS FOR EXPLORATION:

1. Which stressors were depicted?

2. How were the lifelines drawn and how are they useful?

3. How many lifelines did you include?

4. Do you think you have enough lifelines?

5. Which lifeline(s) do you tend to utilize the most?

Vacation Spot in a Box

ADDITIONAL MATERIALS: Small, shallow gifts boxes (about the size of a department store jewelry box).

PROCEDURE: Draw a vacation spot you can visit in order to distance yourself from stress. The spot may be realistic, such as a country cabin or your backyard, or an imaginary place, such as a floating cloud or a magical island. It can be a place you have visited before or a place that you would like to visit in the future.

Create your drawing within the box as a way to contain it. Keep your drawing simple.

BENEFITS: Drawing within the box supports structure and security. In addition, the box may be thought of as a personal gift that you can view whenever you need a break from stress. You can use it as a stress reduction tool when you are away from home and need a reminder of comfort, hope, and stability.

QUESTIONS FOR EXPLORATION:

1. What type of place did you draw? Have you visited this place before? Was your visit effective in terms of stress reduction?

2. How can a break from stress be beneficial to your body and mind?

3. When was the last time you chose to release your stress for a while?

4. Do you deserve a retreat from your anxiety?

Extinguishing Negativity

PROCEDURE: Draw your own unique fire extinguisher to symbolize ways you can target and extinguish the negativity and other things you'd like removed from your life. You may choose to add strong streams of water, foam, powder, compressed nitrogen, or some other material being released from the extinguisher.

BENEFITS: Creating your own extinguisher allows you to release anger, stress, and anxiety by reminding you that you can let go off (and "extinguish") negative thoughts and feelings. It helps you consider what techniques you can use to cope with negativity, such as allowing yourself to say "no," reframing distorted thinking patterns, ridding yourself of toxic relationships, and/or changing your lifestyle.

QUESTIONS FOR EXPLORATION:

1. How would you describe the extinguisher? Does it seem effective?

2. Does the extinguisher need to be upgraded in any way?

3. What types of things in your life need extinguishing?

4. What will you do once you feel freer and your environment is less toxic?

Worry Stones

PROCEDURE: Using any type of soft, non-toxic clay, form a small ball, about half the size of a golf ball. Once it is smooth, press your thumb in it until the bottom of the ball becomes flattened. It should look like a mini trinket tray (just large enough to place a ring in) with the edges rising up just a little bit. Let it dry for a day and then paint it if desired.

BENEFITS: When the item is dry, you can rub your thumb on it as needed whenever you feel anxious. It will help soothe you and serve as a distraction.

QUESTIONS FOR EXPLORATION:

1. How can symbolic items, rituals, or certain patterns of thinking help decrease stress?

2. Do you currently have a special friend, partner, style of thinking, mindfulness technique, or object that helps you reduce anxiety?

3. Which techniques – such as deep breathing, yoga, and meditation – are you presently practicing in order to reduce stress?

A Calm, Peaceful Place

PROCEDURE: Create a relaxing, attractive environment, such as a tropical oasis, that you can escape to when you are stressed. Examples may include your backyard, a lovely park, or the beach. This place may be real or imaginary. You may draw, paint, and/or use collage materials such as cut paper, magazine photos, sequins and stones.

BENEFITS: This is a creative and effective way to reduce stress and focus on positive imagery. It is helpful to be able to visualize a serene scene in order to help you reduce anxiety. Visualizing tranquil imagery may also help you fall asleep quicker.

QUESTIONS FOR EXPLORATION:

1. How can this type of environment be helpful?

2. Do you ever allow yourself to retreat from your work and stress?

3. When was the last time you gave yourself a vacation from your worries?

CLIENT RESPONSE:

A 51-year-old woman named Jane painted an imaginary garden that looked like her actual garden at home. She stated that working on the painting gave her a reprieve from a very stressful day, helped her focus, and made her feel tranquil. Jane shared that her home garden was her refuge from anxiety, chaos, and a pending divorce. She stated that she felt "an amazing transformation" when she spent time there.

Surfing the Wave

PROCEDURE: Draw yourself riding a wave. In dialectical behavioral therapy, "riding the wave" is a technique that allows individuals to deal with uncomfortable thoughts and feelings.[8] The wave begins slowly, peaks, and then dissipates. The idea is to surf the wave (e.g., your discomfort) until it slowly disappears, you feel calm once again, and the anxiety fades away – like the ebb and flow of the ocean.

BENEFITS: By imagining yourself riding your discomfort like you would a wave, this exercise helps you tolerate stress and anxiety, and it increases emotional strength and acceptance. It serves as a reminder not to fight difficult emotions but, rather, to ride them until they fade back into the ocean.

QUESTIONS FOR EXPLORATION:

1. How are you riding the wave (e.g., surfboard, small boat, body surfing, etc.)?
2. How does it feel to surf the wave?
3. What are the advantages to riding it?
4. How can you relate riding the wave to controlling anxiety and stress?

Ship in the Storm

PROCEDURE: Fold a piece of paper into three parts. In the first part, draw a ship entering a storm. In the second part, draw the ship in the storm, and in the third part, draw the ship after the storm. Think of the ship as representing you in some way.

BENEFITS: Engaging in this exercise affords you the opportunity to explore how you act in times of stress, and if your actions help or hurt you. It reminds you that when you feel like you are drowning, you can "surf the waves" and use your coping tools to stay afloat. Remembering the affirmation "This too shall pass" can help you manage adversity.

QUESTIONS FOR EXPLORATION:

1. In which ways does the ship represent aspects of your personality, mood, and determination or lack thereof?
2. How would you describe the way the ship handled the storm?
3. Which part of the picture was the easiest to draw? Most difficult?
4. How did you depict the storm? Was it ferocious or mild? Was there much damage?
5. What was the ocean like? Were there large waves or great gusts of wind?

chapter four

happiness

Happiness is a sense of well-being, joy, or contentment. When people are successful, safe, or lucky, they feel happiness.[1] Research in the field of positive psychology has long since demonstrated that engaging in activities that give us a sense of purpose and meaning, and that reflect our values in life, are associated with the greatest levels of life satisfaction, as they give us a sense of living in accordance with our best self. When we engage in meaningful and value-laden activities, we feel like we are making a difference and that we count.

When I ask clients in therapy groups the question, "What is happiness?" I usually receive many different answers. For some people, the answer is related to mental or physical health, and for others, it involves maintaining financial security, interacting with their family, finding a partner, feeling like their "old self," being independent, spending time with their pet, or going on vacation. The older individuals with whom I work will often joke that happiness is "waking up in the morning."

However you define happiness, there are some certainties. First, you can't solely depend on others for your happiness. Rather, happiness is a disposition that comes from within. Second, there is no magic wand for happiness; it won't become part of your lifestyle unless you nourish and cultivate it. Third, money alone won't produce happiness, and neither will a fancy car or large home.

In addition, happiness appears to be a trait that is at least, in part, influenced by genetics. For example, in her book, *The How of Happiness,* psychologist Sonja Lyubomirsky describes that we all have a "happiness set point," or a baseline level from which our happiness oscillates and then returns to its preset equilibrium. She suggests that 50% of happiness is genetically predetermined, while 10% is due to life circumstances, and 40% is the result of our own personal outlook.[2]

However, this happiness set point is not necessarily fixed in nature, as there are choices that you can make in order to improve your overall feelings of well-being. For example, engaging in gratitude practices, choosing to look at the bright side of life, practicing self-compassion, and learning to "go with the flow" can all increase happiness. In addition, engaging in creative activities, like drawing, painting, journaling, and writing poetry, can help promote a more positive mindset. In fact, research suggests that journaling for 15 minutes a day can increase happiness because it provides an outlet from which you can express yourself and resolve any conflicts or problems.[3] Indeed, people who think creatively tend to be more content. This does not mean that you have to paint like Picasso; it merely involves having a broad perspective on life, empathizing with others, appreciating the beauty in art and nature, and reinventing yourself as needed. It may mean thinking outside the box and taking healthy risks.

When you are able to makes choices that increase your happiness, you are more likely to pursue your goals, stop comparing yourself to others, and allow yourself to be "good enough." In turn, you can stop becoming a victim of your circumstances. You can experience loss, illness, or financial problems and still be an overall happy person. You can learn that problems and obstacles do not have to rule out happiness, and that you can keep experimenting with ways to cope and feel better. You can take healthy risks, tame negative thoughts, and treat yourself with love and respect.

The following exercises are intended to help individuals cultivate a more positive mindset and find the joy in life. Engaging in these practices is associated with a variety of benefits, as happiness is associated with increased longevity, better immune system functioning, improved self-esteem, and enhanced motivation. In addition, people who are brighter and optimistic tend to be better parents, neighbors, and workers.

Gratitude Totem Pole

PROCEDURE: Create a gratitude totem pole of people who have affected you positively in the past, and who currently support you and lift your spirits. You may use photos, sketches, paint, or pieces of paper to create your totem pole. It may be abstract or realistic, or a combination of the two art styles.

BENEFITS: Engaging in gratitude practices can help you create a positive mindset that counteracts stress and depression. It helps you appreciate what you have in life as opposed to focusing on what is missing. Gratitude makes you realize what is truly important and reminds you to appreciate your treasures and count your blessings.

QUESTIONS FOR EXPLORATION:

1. To whom or for what do you feel most grateful?

2. Is your totem pole rich and full, moderate, or leaning toward sparse and empty?

3. Does your structure reflect important people in your life?

4. Is your totem pole a work in progress, or do you believe it is complete?

5. Would it be helpful to view this structure on occasion?

6. Is there anything in your artwork that surprised you? Did you leave anything or anyone out of it?

> "Wear gratitude like a cloak and it will feed every corner of your life."
>
> – Rumi

Affirmation Tree to Grow Self-Worth

PROCEDURE: Draw the outline of a tree, including a number of large leaves.[4] Place some of your favorite affirmations on the leaves and fill the tree in with color. Colored pencils work well for this project. Spend time observing your artwork and explore the positive feelings derived from examining and reciting the affirmations. The following are some examples of affirmations:

- "I am enough."

- "I will do my best and then leave myself alone."

- "I will accomplish my goals."

- "I am abundantly joyful and happy."

- "I am so grateful for my life."

- "I am fine just as I am."

BENEFITS: Repeating affirmations reminds you to look at the positive side of life and focus on your strengths. Focusing on the positive enhances feelings of happiness, gratitude, and self-worth. With practice, the regular use of positive affirmations may eventually become second nature to you, and can lead to healthier thinking, improved mood, and more productive behavior.

QUESTIONS FOR EXPLORATION:

1. Does your tree represent your current mood, feelings, or self-worth?

2. Are there many leaves on your tree, a moderate amount, or just a few?

3. Which leaves were emphasized artistically, and which leaves are most motivating?

4. How can affirmations help you feel happier about yourself and your life now?

A Little Bit of Joy

PROCEDURE: Create a sketch or collage of the "little things" in life that presently give you joy or have given you joy in the past. Examples may include: your morning cup of coffee or tea, coffee breaks during the work day, brief naps, your favorite foods, petting your dog or cat, a sunrise or sunset, babies, a vacation, relaxation, the beach, watching sports, listening to music, a hug from a friend, a smile from someone you love, art, or a special family gathering.

BENEFITS: Life satisfaction, happiness, and self-worth are increased when you remind yourself of the pleasures that life has to offer. By recalling fond memories of the small things that give you joy, you can enhance gratitude, self-acceptance, and emotional resilience.

QUESTIONS FOR EXPLORATION:

1. What is your reaction upon viewing your artwork?

2. Which "little things" are most significant?

3. Are there any items symbolized in your artwork that you take for granted or have forgotten about?

4. Is there anything depicted that you can resume doing or appreciating?

5. Are there any images or symbols in your artwork that represent people, places, or things that have played a role in who you are today?

Popsicle Stick Affirmations

ADDITIONAL MATERIALS: Large popsicle sticks or tongue depressors.

PROCEDURE: Write an affirmation on a popsicle stick and decorate it if desired. Once you are finished, place your stick in a container in the middle of the table, after which each group member will select one stick and read it aloud. When everyone has shared, you may keep the affirmation stick you chose.

BENEFITS: Reciting and exploring the meaning of positive affirmations serves to increase self-worth and enhance motivation, and it helps you develop a more positive outlook on life.

QUESTIONS FOR EXPLORATION:

1. What is your reaction to the affirmation you chose? Are you able to incorporate its message into your everyday life?

2. How does the affirmation relate to your thought processes, behavior, lifestyle, and/or attitudes?

3. Do you have your own favorite affirmation? Which affirmation did you write on your original popsicle stick?

4. How can positive thoughts and statements improve your mood, self-esteem, and quality of life?

Controlling Negative Thoughts

PROCEDURE: *Provide group members with the outline of a person's profile, or ask them to design their own profile that takes up much of a 8½ × 11 inch page.* Within the profile, draw or list any worries and negative thoughts that you focus on frequently. Next, on a separate piece of paper, sketch a variety of small, positive symbols, such as suns, rainbows, flowers, hearts, and smiling faces. Then, cut out the positive sketches and use them to cover up the negative symbols and words that compose the profile (glue or tape may be used).

BENEFITS: Engaging in this exercise allows you to take symbolic control over your negative thoughts and worries. It also helps you become aware of your thinking patterns and gives you the power to control negativity by consciously transforming it into positive thinking. Happiness begins when you overcome worry and conquer your "doom and gloom" attitude.

QUESTIONS FOR EXPLORATION:

1. How many negative thoughts were covered? Which negative thoughts did you cover?

2. How did the "cover up" make you feel?

3. What message does your profile convey to you?

4. Share one or more ways you can brighten unpleasant thoughts you are having today.

5. When was the last time you attempted to change unhealthy thinking styles?

Filling a Mug with Happiness

PROCEDURE: Design a painting or drawing of a large mug, and fill it with images, colors, and shapes that give you a sense of joy. Examples may include an image of a sun, moon, flower, heart, fireworks, beach, cake, or party.

BENEFITS: Engaging in this exercise reminds you to focus on the positive. When you are mindful of everyday pleasures and concentrate as much as possible on joyful thoughts and experiences, you can lift your mood and increase your sense of well-being and motivation.

QUESTIONS FOR EXPLORATION:

1. How full is your mug?

2. Is there anything missing from the mug?

3. Was there anything that filled your mug *in the past* that is missing now?

4. Are you satisfied with the contents?

5. Is there anything you would like to add now or in the future?

Experiencing a Burst of Joy

PROCEDURE: Depict the feeling you experience (or may possibly experience in the future) when you have a burst of joy following a splendid event, such as the birth of a baby, being the guest of honor at a surprise party, watching an amazing sunrise or sunset, winning the lottery, falling in love, being given a substantial raise, or being unexpectedly invited on a special vacation.

BENEFITS: Sometimes, we become so used to sadness, worry, and gloom that we forget what it may feel like to enjoy life. Getting in touch with happiness and the feelings, colors, movements, and shapes associated with it can be very healing and insightful.

QUESTIONS FOR EXPLORATION:

1. What does your burst look like? Is it colorful? Does it fill the page? Is it full of movement?

2. When was the last time you felt true bliss?

3. How can you tailor your environment so you can experience pleasure more often?

Happy Words for Living

PROCEDURE: Write at least five happy words on a piece of paper and illustrate them in any way you desire to create an integrated design consisting of symbols, images, words, and shapes. Some examples of happy words include: peace, love, caring, mindfulness, gratitude, family, hope, smile, laughter, closeness, beauty, babies, believe, serenity, and inspiration.

BENEFITS: When you list and then symbolize uplifting words, positive feelings are often elicited. Reciting and living in accordance with positivity lifts the spirit and soul. It decreases sadness as it increases motivation and self-worth.

QUESTIONS FOR EXPLORATION:

1. Which words and designs represent joy? What are your associations to the images in the artwork?

2. How can you start to focus on positivity?

3. When was the last time you began or ended the day with positive statements, such as, "I am at peace," "I am grateful for…," or "I am proud of myself"?

Building Blocks of Happiness

PROCEDURE: Draw at least four or more squares, one placed on top of the other, and fill them in with things you need to achieve happiness in your life. For example, one block may contain a heart to represent love and another may contain children to symbolize the need for a close family.

BENEFITS: Identification of wants and needs, and exploration of ways to achieve them, is the first step toward fulfilling lifelong and/or more recent goals, hopes and dreams.

QUESTIONS FOR EXPLORATION:

1. Which blocks are most significant?

2. Do you already have something in your life that is represented in one of the blocks? For example, are you already enjoying love in your life now?

3. What steps can you take to get your needs met?

4. Are there any blocks that are unrealistic? If so, are you able to tolerate that these wishes will not happen? Are you able to make substitutions that are more credible?

5. What role does hope play in building or re-building your blocks of happiness?

6. How high would you like the blocks to reach? Would you like to achieve a tower or skyscraper, or is a small structure satisfactory?

You Choose Your Happiness

PROCEDURE: Draw a figure throwing a lasso around a symbol of happiness. A lasso is typically drawn as a rope with a circular ring at the end of it, which is meant to catch something (typically cattle or horses). Examples of things you might lasso to find happiness include a heart to represent love, children to symbolize family, a smiling face to represent a sense of humor, or dollar bills to represent financial freedom.

BENEFITS: Similar to throwing a lasso, this exercise reminds you to keep your eyes open wide, look around, and throw your energy toward that which brings you happiness. It reminds you that you need to take charge of your life if you want to feel satisfied. In most cases, people can choose to pursue happiness, or at least accept their lot in life, but attitude is key. Happiness usually involves making the conscious decision to engage in daily practices that bring you peace and joy and that contribute toward a life worth living.

QUESTIONS FOR EXPLORATION:

1. What are you lassoing and in what manner are you trying to catch your object?

2. In your artwork, have you caught what you were pursuing?

3. What type of lasso did you draw? Is it sturdy, weak, long, or short?

4. Are you skilled in using it?

5. What happens when you catch your desired person, place, or thing?

CLIENT RESPONSE:

A 91-year-old woman named Lilly, shared that she was trying to lasso acceptance of her life situation. She remarked that she felt sad for losses in her life and for her inability to do the things she was able to do when she was younger. She said she still tries to be thankful and feels grateful that she is alive and not in pain. She stated that she likes to eat all her meals and she sleeps well. Lilly shared that she enjoys being in her little home and appreciates her helpers who keep her house tidy and assist her in dressing and cooking. Lilly's motto was, "What is, is, and what was, was." She relayed this saying in Yiddish to group members who tried to repeat it, albeit unsuccessfully. They smiled, though, getting the gist of what Lilly was conveying to them.

Happiness Map

PROCEDURE: In the center of the page, draw something in your life that elicits happiness. This center will be your starting point. From there, use lines, shapes, and branch-like structures to connect the people, places, animals, positive thoughts, or memories that bring you happiness. Create as many connections to the original symbol as possible.

BENEFITS: Getting in touch with that which gives you pleasure enhances feelings of happiness, promotes a positive attitude, and increases motivation. By creating a map of the things in your life that bring you happiness, you can decrease stress and anxiety, and strengthen physical and emotional health.

QUESTIONS FOR EXPLORATION:

1. What does your map represent about your life and yourself?

2. Are there any changes you would like to make regarding what is placed on your map?

3. Was your map different in the past, and do you think it will change in the future?

4. How simple or complicated is your map?

CLIENT RESPONSE:

A 25-year-old man named Justin, healing from a deep depression and trying to overcome an addiction to marijuana, drew the base of his happiness as a Starbucks cup of coffee. He stated that he begins every day with a large macchiato and shared that his coffee is usually the highlight of his day. He remarked the rest of his day usually "sucks." He did add positive words to his map, some of which included "family," "music," "singing," "exercise," "my girlfriend," "friends," and "pizza." Justin also added a dark black question mark to the center of the map, which he shared represented the unknown, as he did not know what would keep him from feeling depressed and hopeless again in the future.

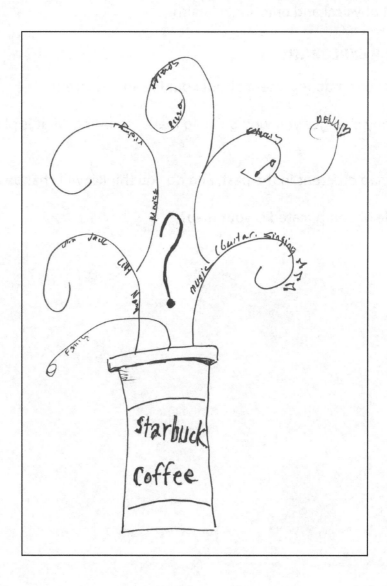

Patterns of Joy

PROCEDURE: Create a pattern design that instills brightness and cheer. Think about repetitive shapes, images, and figures in movement as you create your design. For example, you may create a repeating pattern involving an arrangement of flowers, hearts, sunrises and sunsets, smiling faces, or figures dancing. You can also include words and magazine photos in your creation.

BENEFITS: Drawing happiness distracts you from dwelling on sad or negative thoughts. It reminds you to choose positive thinking when you have enough strength to make that choice. The act of drawing cheerful art increases your focus, purpose, mindset, and self-awareness.

QUESTIONS FOR EXPLORATION:

1. Which patterns represent your current thinking? How do the patterns represent the way you would like to see yourself, life, and the world?

2. Do your thinking patterns tend to remain about the same, or do they change frequently or periodically?

3. How does the way you think affect your mood, motivation, and behavior?

4. Have your thinking patterns changed over the years?

Happiness Machine

PROCEDURE: Draw a machine, with a variety of parts, that will help increase joy in your life. As you create your machine, think of designing it like a Rube Goldberg machine, which is a device that uses a complex chain reaction to complete a simple task in an overly complicated manner. Each step in the machine triggers the next step, like a domino effect, until the task is complete.[5]

BENEFITS: This creative exercise facilitates problem solving and promotes feelings of lightheartedness as you examine different methods you can use to increase pleasure and decrease sadness and stress. In addition, this artistic technique helps you understand that, sometimes, you have to take many small steps in order to achieve your goals. There is no specific formula or method; we each have to find our own specific path to happiness.

QUESTIONS FOR EXPLORATION:

1. How does your machine work? What steps are involved in pursuing the goal of happiness?

2. Which steps seem to be the easiest? Which ones seem to be the most difficult?

3. Do you think happiness can be achieved? How long do you think it will take to achieve at least part of your goal?

4. How does taking small steps toward your objective help?

5. Which part of your machine is most unique? Which part will be most advantageous to your current needs?

CLIENT RESPONSE:

A 29-year-old man named Sal drew a machine that would "soothe you before bed." He stated that it consisted of many parts, including his iPhone®, which would play soothing music for about an hour. A switch from the phone would connect to a light switch in his bedroom, which would dim the lights and close the blinds. A battery under his bed would create a gentle swaying movement. A long metal arm with a life-like hand would provide a glass of milk or a mug of hot chocolate and cookies or crackers. Finally, a soft blanket placed on the bed would heat up a little bit "to make you feel warm and comfortable." Sal shared that the most important part of this machine was that it would be distributed to everyone for free, so that most people could benefit from a good night's sleep. Sal remarked that if he could get a good night's sleep, he would feel less angry and irritable all the time.

Mandala Full of Hope

PROCEDURE: Using a paper plate, make an outline of a circle to form a mandala. Then, fill it in with sketches that represent what hope means to you and what you are hopeful for in the future. Create images that reflect your expectations, wishes, goals, and desires (e.g., to be in a relationship, own a home, graduate from college, etc.).

BENEFITS: Focusing on hope enhances motivation and creates a positive attitude. When you have faith in yourself and in your future, you are better able to concentrate and problem solve. It allows you to identify and pursue realistic, purposeful, and constructive goals. It gives you something to look forward to and strive for daily.

QUESTIONS FOR EXPLORATION:

1. What did you symbolize within your mandala?

2. How is hope represented?

3. How does having faith motivate you? Do you feel driven now?

4. Are your wishes feasible?

5. Do you have a plan as to how you can achieve these objectives?

CLIENT RESPONSE:

Tom, a 46-year-old podiatrist recovering from depression and addiction issues, designed this peaceful looking "Mandala of Hope." Tom remarked, "Hope is all I have right now." He shared that he was recently divorced after 16 years of marriage and lost his job and driver's license because of his drinking problem; he had very little money left in his bank account. He was forced to move out of his comfortable home and was renting a room in a small run-down townhouse.

He stated his wish was to get his job back, which he knew could take as long as two years, and to feel a sense of belonging again. Tom remarked he wanted to have a family, and he wanted to have a child before "He was too old to procreate." Tom sighed while reviewing his art work, sharing that he needed to find his purpose again and would try to "hang on."

Currently, he viewed his lack of finances as his greatest problem because he didn't have enough money to eat in a nutritious manner (he was overweight and diabetic) and he didn't have a way to get to his AA meetings because he couldn't afford an Uber or taxi. Tom did say that drawing and designing this mandala helped him relax, even just for a short while. He viewed art therapy as "a safe place where he could be himself."

Humor Collagette

PROCEDURE: Design a collagette of people, places, thoughts, memories, and experiences that put a smile on your face. Some examples of humorous designs that you might incorporate in your collagette include: a photo of someone making silly faces, a picture of a baby playing with her food while it's splattered all over her face, symbols and images representing humorous experiences or memories, or your own drawings of unusual looking people, animals, or creatures.

BENEFITS: We sometimes get angry over things that are silly or unimportant in the long run. This humorous exercise helps put things into perspective by reminding you not to always take yourself so seriously. In addition, laughter can be considered a workout for your body, as it has been shown to decrease stress and blood pressure, boost your immune system, relieve pain, increase energy, and, in some studies, it has even been shown to increase cognitive abilities.

QUESTIONS FOR EXPLORATION:

1. Which part of your artwork attracts your attention the most?

2. Which is the funniest part of your work?

3. How does humor seem to help you?

4. What types of movies, videos, people, thoughts, etc., do you find comical?

5. When was the last time you had a good belly laugh?

Strips of Gratitude

PROCEDURE: Cut a variety of paper into strips of varying sizes and write or symbolize what you are grateful for on each strip. Place the strips on a white or colored sheet of paper in any way you like to create a personal design.

BENEFITS: Gratitude allows you to take stock of the positive aspects of your life and to acknowledge what is special about your relationships, work, and everyday existence. It lowers anxiety and depression and increases satisfaction and motivation.

QUESTIONS FOR EXPLORATION:

1. What are you most grateful for in your life?

2. How does gratitude provide relief from stress?

3. Which strips attract your attention the most?

4. Are there any gratitude strips you hope to include in the future? Are there any strips you may have left out unintentionally or intentionally?

5. Are you able to relate the design you created to the way gratitude currently colors your life?

Beauty and the Beads

ADDITIONAL MATERIALS: Thin, stretchy beading material (that can be easily knotted) and inexpensive, colorful beads with wider holes for easy threading.

PROCEDURE: Examine the beads and choose ones that attract you or make you feel cheerful. Then, make a bracelet, necklace, or other item (e.g., a simple knotted chain of beads). When your beaded creation is complete, share your work with the group and give it a special, positive meaning. For example, a bracelet may be considered a "bracelet of hope," or it may be thought of as an "I love myself bracelet" or an "I am fine as I am bracelet." Similarly, a chain of beads may be considered a "mindfulness chain" to help you remember to take deep breaths and use coping skills. This way, whenever you wear the item, you will be reminded of its significance.

BENEFITS: This exercise helps to reduce stress, and also brings self-awareness and increased self-esteem. The process of choosing and then creating your personal trinket or piece of jewelry inspires positivity and strength. Designing this type of art is soothing and therapeutic because it promotes mindfulness and enhances one's focus. Creating something special for yourself or others is empowering and provides you with a sense of purpose.

QUESTIONS FOR EXPLORATION:

1. What is the significance of the item you designed?

2. How can it help when you feel stressed or unworthy?

3. How did it feel to design the item, and what is the significance of the beads you chose?

4. Did you tend to choose brighter or darker beads? Larger or smaller beads? Does your completed work relate to your mood, feeling, or personality characteristics?

Draw Your "Bounce"

PROCEDURE: Create a drawing, painting, or collage of your "bounce." Your bounce can be considered your level of energy, motivation, and happiness. Think about its size, movement, and shape. When considering what your bounce looks like, you may even think of Tigger in the *Winnie the Pooh*® series.

BENEFITS: This creative exercise increases self-awareness with regard to your energy levels, behavior patterns, and enthusiasm.

QUESTIONS FOR EXPLORATION:

1. How did you draw your "bounce"? Do you have one right now?

2. Was it easy, moderate, or difficult to portray your bounce?

3. How high is it?

4. What types of colors, images, and shapes are included in your design?

5. Do you notice movement, flow, or patterns?

6. What is most distinctive about it?

Attributes within a Figure

PROCEDURE: Draw the outline of a person that covers most of the page. *The group leader can also distribute an outline of the human form to those who desire more structure.* Imagine that this figure represents yourself, and fill it in with upbeat, constructive words, attributes, strengths, and achievements. You may use artistic symbols, magazine photos, images, sketches, and phrases to fill your figure.

BENEFITS: Sometimes we forget or ignore how strong and capable we are, and how important we are to people in our environment, such as family, friends, neighbors and co-workers. When we explore and acknowledge our positive attributes and achievements, it is therapeutic and enlightening. This project allows us to do that in a peaceful, non-threatening manner.

QUESTIONS FOR EXPLORATION:

1. In which ways is the figure self-representative?

2. How do you feel about the figure's appearance and its "filling"?

3. Is the figure complete?

4. Is there more that needs to be added?

5. How would you characterize the figure?

6. How does viewing it make you feel?

7. If it could speak, what do you think it may say to you?

Re-Defining Happiness

PROCEDURE: *Before beginning this activity, the group leader will discuss how our definition of happiness may need to be transformed during different periods of our life, depending on our age, situation, and experiences. For example, the loss of a loved one or a long-time job may push us to create another way of finding joy and fulfillment.*

Draw ways in which you can redefine happiness for yourself. For example, someone who used to love being a professional dancer and now is retired may draw a sketch of herself dancing with tots to represent that she has found a new type of joy teaching children to dance.

BENEFITS: This exercise helps you explore the process of change and the way that people adjust to life's circumstances. It helps you explore new ways to find pleasure and consider innovative methods to reinvent yourself. It highlights the importance of making the most of what you have and are capable of doing.

QUESTIONS FOR EXPLORATION:

1. Have you needed to redefine your definition of happiness recently or in the past? How challenging was this to do and how long did it take?

2. How does using our physical and emotional strength help us to make transformations and changes as needed?

3. How does your sketch represent a redefining of happiness for you?

Waves of Gratitude

PROCEDURE: Draw a series of waves, and sketch small symbols of people, places, and things that you are grateful for on or in between the waves. Try to relate the color, size, and strength of the waves to the amount of gratitude you feel. For example, a large, brightly colored wave representing gratitude for family might stand out more than a smaller, less colorful wave that symbolizes gratitude for your job.

BENEFITS: Gratitude has been shown to increase positivity, self-esteem, and motivation. It may help you sleep better, reduce anxiety and depression, boost your immune system, and generally feel better. This exercise helps you to acknowledge and appreciate commonplace experiences and simple pleasures, such as a sunrise or the feel of the wind on your cheeks, as well as material items like your computer or other new technology. It helps us realize the importance of people, places, and things we may take for granted (e.g., family members, friends, close neighbors, etc.).

QUESTIONS FOR EXPLORATION:

1. Which waves are most significant?

2. Which feelings are elicited upon viewing the various waves?

3. How does gratitude help you gain a healthier perspective about your life?

4. What are you most thankful for today?

Tree of Mind

PROCEDURE: Draw a pine tree or a tree that resembles a Christmas tree. *The group leader may also provide an outline of a pine tree for participants who desire more structure.* Next, place a variety of ornaments on the tree that represent the positivity in your life. The top ornament, where the star would normally be placed, should represent the most positive thing in your life, with the ornaments descending in significance from there.

BENEFITS: This exercise helps you gain a better understanding of, and appreciation for, what is most important in life. It helps you develop increased optimism, gratitude, and greater awareness of your gifts as you design the tree and its adornments.

QUESTIONS FOR EXPLORATION:

1. What is placed at the top of the tree, and what is its meaning for you?

2. Which other ornaments have deep significance for you?

3. How is your tree designed? Does it seem festive, or is it in need of decoration?

4. How does your tree represent your mood and feelings?

5. In retrospect, were you aware of all the positive things in your life?

Shapes of Unconditional Love

PROCEDURE: Draw a large heart or whatever shape you desire that signifies love and joy to you. Within it, sketch realistic or abstract images of people, places, pets, ideas, or beliefs that provide you with unconditional love. For example, you may decide to include your dog, family members, religion, nature, or art in your sketch.

BENEFITS: This activity promotes increased feelings of love, self-worth, and value. Having people and other things in our life that provide us with unconditional love helps us better deal with challenges and helps us focus and remain calmer in times of stress. When we feel valued, our self-esteem and motivation increases, and we are more likely to persevere in the face of adversity.

QUESTIONS FOR EXPLORATION:

1. What does unconditional love mean to you?

2. Who or what provides you with unconditional love? If you can't think of anything now, are you able to think of someone or something in the past that filled that need?

3. Do you love someone or something unconditionally? Has your devotion ever been tested?

4. How does knowing there is someone or something that loves you without reservation help you handle life's challenges?

5. What are specific ways you can bring this powerful love to your awareness when you feel depressed or when your emotional mind seems to dominate your thoughts?

In the Palm of My Hand

PROCEDURE: Sketch your hand or trace the outline your hand. As you draw, think about the phrase, "It's in the palm of my hand," which means, "I have this under control." Within the hand outline, illustrate one or more things you feel confident about. For example, you may feel confident about your ability to take care of your health, and your ability to excel at school or at your job. You may be a supportive friend or family member, and take pride in doing well at sports such as baseball, swimming, golf or tennis.

BENEFITS: Although there are some things in life that are out of your control, this exercise helps increase your awareness of what *is* in your control. It helps you focus on your strengths, which can increase positive feelings and enhance your confidence.

QUESTIONS FOR EXPLORATION:

1. What are you in control of now? How does that feel?

2. How can you gain increased control of other areas of your life?

3. What techniques can you utilize to help you focus on your strengths as opposed to your perceived weaknesses?

Personal Freedom

PROCEDURE: *Group leaders should provide participants with a variety of bird templates for this exercise.* Either outline or make a copy of the various bird templates in front of you, and then cut each one out and glue it on a sheet of white paper. Next, fill in the bird outlines with images, shapes, colors, words, affirmations, and magazine photos that represent what personal freedom means to you.

BENEFITS: Participating in this exercise helps you acknowledge the importance of leading a life that is meaningful and purposeful *for you*. You don't have to make important choices – such as whether or not to attend college, marry, have children, pursue a specific career, or live in a particular state, city, or neighborhood – solely to please someone else or society at large. Your freedom is, "The right to be who you want to be, not what other people expect or want you to be."[6]

QUESTIONS FOR EXPLORATION:

1. What is your definition of freedom?

2. How is freedom related to feelings of peace and happiness?

3. How is freedom represented in your artwork?

4. Are you ready to be more independent? What may be standing in your way?

5. Would you like to have the freedom that birds seem to have? How would life be different if you felt more liberated?

CLIENT RESPONSE:

A 36-year-old woman named Claire chose to draw one bird flying over a mountain range, "without a care in the world." Claire shared that freedom for her would mean having the ability to do what she wanted, when she wanted, and "most importantly," having the money to travel anywhere in the world. She shared that she wanted to visit Rocky Mountain National Park and see the rest of the United States before traveling abroad. Claire remarked that she doubted she would have the opportunity to follow this dream since she was in debt and stuck in a dead-end job that she hated. She stated that the only freedom she experienced was on Sundays, when she was able to sleep late and plan her day. Claire moaned that she worked six days a week and was exhausted by the time she arrived home each evening.

Passions That Energize

PROCEDURE: Draw things you are passionate about within a shape of your choosing. The shape may be spontaneously drawn, or it may be self-representative (e.g., the shape of the state in which you were born, or a shape that symbolizes your current mood, such as a heart or cloud). Some examples of passions that you may include in your shape are your children, grandchildren, pets, hobbies, work, art, music, poetry, sports, or certain causes, like reducing global warming.

BENEFITS: Increasing awareness of your passions and interests can help you become more positive, optimistic, and motivated. People who actively pursue passions often have more energy, better immune systems, and are rarely bored. They find it easier to deal with problems, and many individuals seem to have less difficulty rising in the morning, even knowing there are challenges ahead.

QUESTIONS FOR EXPLORATION:

1. Which activities do you find energizing?

2. Is there any activity you used to pursue, but have ignored or forgotten about recently?

3. What may stand in your way of engaging in pleasing activities?

4. Which personality characteristics seem to change when you participate in purposeful and stimulating pursuits?

Positivity Mask

ADDITIONAL MATERIALS: Masks and collage materials, such as sequins and pom-poms.

PROCEDURE: Design a mask using positive images, photos, colors, shapes, words, phrases, and affirmations. It may reflect any part of your personality, and/or hopes, dreams and goals.

BENEFITS: This activity focuses on happiness, strengths, self-compassion, and positivity. This type of mask design provides you with the opportunity to tune into your thoughts and feelings, and to focus on brightness, your strengths, and optimism. You can celebrate your unique characteristics in a creative and personal manner.

QUESTIONS FOR EXPLORATION:

1. Does the mask or part of the mask reflect your mood, attitude, or feelings of self-worth?

2. What part of the mask attracts you the most?

3. Which part is most inspirational?

4. What are the benefits of thinking in a positive manner?

5. When was the last time you felt hopeful or were motivated to pursue a goal?

6. What is one thing you can do today to motivate yourself to think in a brighter manner?

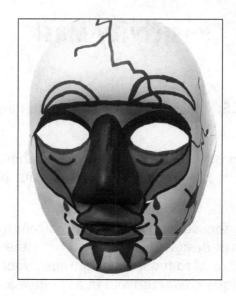

CLIENT RESPONSE:

Eddie, a 32-year-old man with bipolar disorder, designed this vibrant, abstract mask. He shared that the outside of the mask is bright and colorful, but underneath the brightness lies a dark, gloomy depression (see the tears and jagged scar-like lines on the head). Eddies related the mask to himself in that he smiles and jokes a lot, but at home he is usually depressed, anxious, and frightened. He stated that he has considered self-harm many times, but his wife, whom he adores, is very supportive and accepting, and helps give him a reason to "stay here."

Gratitude: Healthy Food for Your Mind

PROCEDURE: Draw a picture of a picnic spread on the ground in a park, field, garden, forest, or yard. On the picnic blanket, draw symbols or add words representing people, places, and things for which you feel grateful. These will represent the "food" that is a metaphor for your blessings. Examples may include your family, your friends, your home, pets, or a beating heart to represent health and vitality.

BENEFITS: "Gratitude is one of the most important foods for the soul, as it has the ability to enhance and maintain happiness and well-being, and this in turn nourishes the mind, body and spirit."[7] When people engage in gratitude practices, they pay attention to what they are thankful for in their lives, as opposed to what they are lacking. It can make them more compassionate toward themselves and others, and it can motivate them to make changes that benefit their well-being and facilitate self-improvement.

QUESTIONS FOR EXPLORATION:

1. What did you place on the picnic blanket? Which "foods" are most nourishing for you?

2. How full is your blanket? Is it a meal fit for a king, or is it rather bare?

3. Do you tend to take time to count your blessings?

4. For what do you feel most thankful?

The Beauty of Flowers

PROCEDURE: Draw a page full of flowers. Feel free to design your own unique variations, which can be realistic, abstract, or both. The flowers may take the form of people or animals, and they may be swaying, dancing, situated in groups, or spaced apart.

BENEFITS: Nature in general elicits many positive thoughts, feelings, and emotions. This exercise helps you tap into several of the following benefits that are derived from appreciating the flowers in the environment:[8]

- **Positive emotions:** Flowers can just sit there and elicit a positive response. When you feel positive, you are more open-minded, creative, and productive.

- **Mental break:** Gazing at flowers can provide you with a mini-break in your day. Even a brief moment with nature allows your mind to rest and restore itself.

- **Appreciation:** When people pass or sit by flowers, they appreciate them. Appreciation is good for the heart, as it brings the heart into a coherent rhythm.

- **Mindfulness:** Taking the time to stop and smell the flowers provides you with a mini-mindfulness break, which can reduce stress and increase clarity.

- **Gratitude:** Simply by being their beautiful selves, flowers give you a reason to be grateful and express your thanks for the beauty in this world.

QUESTIONS FOR EXPLORATION:

1. What types of flowers did you draw? Are any of them self-representative?

2. Are the flowers animated or still?

3. Are they blooming or still buds?

4. Do you have a favorite flower?

5. What feelings are elicited when you gaze at flowers?

> *"The earth laughs in flowers."*
> – Ralph Waldo Emerson

Everyday Life Collagette

ADDITIONAL MATERIALS: A variety of small, everyday objects, such as Band-Aids,® cotton rounds, newspaper coupons, small cereal boxes, Q-Tips®, cotton balls, tea bags, candy wrappers, ticket stubs, and stamps.

PROCEDURE: Create a collagette to represent an artistic portrayal of your everyday life. Glue a variety of small, common objects and magazine photos on a piece of thin cardboard, poster board, or watercolor paper in any way you wish that represent your daily routine. You can include drawings on your collagette as well.

BENEFITS: By exploring your daily routines, patterns of thinking, desires, and genuine needs, you can create a life that is satisfying and comfortable. At times, we may believe that we require more than we have, but in retrospect, it is our thinking that warrants changing, as opposed to our friends, family, or relationships. Occasionally, we may also feel a void and believe that we must fill the void with material objects (e.g., new cars, jewelry, computers, phones); in reality, though, it is a sense of connection or purpose in life that is missing. Therefore, it is helpful to periodically take inventory of your lifestyle, attitudes, and habits so you can determine if changes need to be made to facilitate your happiness and overall well-being.

QUESTIONS FOR EXPLORATION:

1. What do you need to feel content and to lead a healthy lifestyle?

2. How satisfied are you with your daily routine?

3. What do you like most about daily life? What do you like the least?

4. What time of the day is your favorite? Least favorite?

5. How do the items you tend to use most days of the week represent your self-esteem, personality, or attitude? For example, do you tend to spend a lot of time putting makeup on in front of the mirror, or are you glued to your iPhone?

6. Is there anything you are missing in your life?

7. Are you substituting any material items for something that is missing in your life?

8. What do you need today?

Affirmations That Roll

ADDITIONAL MATERIALS: Empty 1.88-inch roll of packing or electrical tape; magazines. The tape roll will look like a thick cardboard bangle bracelet.

PROCEDURE: Cut out a variety of positive symbols, affirmations, and encouraging phrases, and glue them to the outside of the empty tape roll. You can also draw or write your own affirmations if you'd like. The inside of the roll can contain positive affirmations as well, or you can just include a variety of colors and shapes that are appealing to you. Then, allow the tape holder to roll away from you, and enjoy watching the affirmations roll around. Wait to see which affirmation ends up on top.

BENEFITS: Creating a roll of affirmations allows you to view positive symbols and words that uplift your spirits and remind you to "keep going," and to "roll with the punches."

QUESTIONS FOR EXPLORATION:

1. Which affirmation(s) is most inspiring for you?

2. When will the affirmation roll be most helpful?

3. How can taking a lighthearted approach to thinking positively help your overall mood and outlook?

chapter five

self-awareness

With our busy schedules, it might be difficult to think about who we are, our strengths and weaknesses, our drives and personalities, our habits and values. Many people just aren't inclined to spend too much time on self-reflection. Even when personal feedback is presented to us, we're not always open to it.

Self-awareness is important for many reasons. It can improve your judgment and help you identify opportunities for personal growth and professional development. Self-awareness builds self-esteem and confidence. It helps you decide which direction your life should be following and what your needs and desires are.

Being self-aware includes acknowledging and understanding your:

- Wishes and desires
- Strengths
- Weaknesses
- Motivation
- Health and happiness
- Challenges
- Relationships with others
- Barriers to achieving wishes
- Beliefs and values
- Self-esteem

When you are self-aware, you have an understanding of your desires, fears, dreams, and goals. You know what has to be completed in order to head in the right direction and can make a plan to get there. However, being unhappy or indecisive makes it difficult to recognize your purpose, thinking patterns, and life path. In turn, it is more challenging to forge ahead and overcome obstacles. In order to overcome this indecision or stagnancy, you can engage in self-awareness activities, which help create a pathway for further exploration and reflection.

The following exercises are intended to help individuals broaden their outlook and examine their identity, lifestyle, goals, relationships, purpose, and overall sense of life satisfaction. In order for people to change their negative thought patterns, unhealthy behaviors, and low self-esteem, they must first become aware of any barriers to happiness and success.

Two Sides of Me

PROCEDURE: Draw the outline of the front and back of a person that covers most of the page. *The group leader can also distribute an outline of the human form to those who desire more structure.* Then, fill the front of the figure with shapes, images, and words that represent what you are ready to begin exploring and acknowledging about yourself (e.g., your fears, desires, frustrations, shyness, immobility). On the back of the figure, draw or list what you are ready to let go of (e.g., guilt, anger, stress). Next, decorate the rest of the figure and add an environment around it if you desire.

BENEFITS: This exercise may help you gain a better understanding of unhealthy thoughts and harmful interpersonal relationships that you may be clinging to for the wrong reasons. It will help you to observe and examine what you need to do in order to feel better and function more effectively.

QUESTIONS FOR EXPLORATION:

1. What are the main issues you need to explore now?

2. What types of things are you ready to get rid of?

3. What do you notice about the way you filled in the figure? For example, did you use bright colors? Did you add features? Does the figure appear to be smiling or frowning?

4. In which ways does the figure represent your characteristics, thoughts, and feelings?

5. Do you prefer to focus on the front or the back of the figure right now? What are the reasons for your preference?

Collage of Hopes and Wishes

PROCEDURE: Create a collage using your own series of sketches and/or magazine photos representing your hopes and wishes. Examples may include a photo of your dream home, a picture of a smiling person to symbolize a desired relationship, or an office building to represent the job you want in the future.

BENEFITS: This collage can be seen as a mini-vision board that will help you observe and reflect upon your goals. You can come back and reference the collage whenever you need help with motivation, planning, and action.

QUESTIONS FOR EXPLORATION:

1. How motivated do you feel to work toward your goals?

2. Did you add any photos to the collage that you haven't thought of before today?

3. Did you add any photos that surprised you or struck you as extremely positive or negative?

4. Do you believe your dreams are realistic? Are they achievable?

5. What are the first small steps you need to take to work toward your objectives?

Puzzle Pieces of My Life

ADDITIONAL MATERIALS: Assortment of cardboard puzzle pieces (can be found at an art supply store or designed by the group leader).

PROCEDURE: *The group leader should provide an assortment of puzzle pieces for participants to use as templates.* Take the puzzle pieces in front of you and outline them onto a larger piece of white paper until most of the sheet is covered. Next, fill in the puzzle pieces with images, colors, shapes, and words that symbolize the significant parts of your life. These may include achievements, milestones (e.g., marriage, births, graduations), changes (e.g., a move or job promotion), transformations (e.g., weight loss), or lifestyle modifications (e.g., choosing to live simply in a rural setting). *Optional: Participants may fill in the background with colors that relate in some way to their puzzle piece design.*

BENEFITS: It is important to occasionally take inventory of where you are in life and assess what has led to your current circumstances. Reviewing life events helps you sort out problems, take responsibility, acknowledge your strengths, and examine your patterns of behavior. It also helps you understand that you are a product of many experiences, and you have the power to change your life direction and add more positive puzzle pieces if you desire.

QUESTIONS FOR EXPLORATION:

1. Which pieces are most significant?

2. Which parts of the puzzle still affect you now?

3. Are there parts of the puzzle that bring up strong emotions, such as anger or anxiety?

4. Are there parts of the puzzle that have had an impact on your attitude and personality characteristics?

5. Which puzzle parts are you most proud of? Least proud of?

Life as a Rollercoaster

PROCEDURE: Draw your life as if it were a rollercoaster. Think about the complexity, speed, size, and shape of the rollercoaster. Place yourself within the picture if possible.

BENEFITS: It's helpful to periodically assess your life course and the degree of satisfaction or dissatisfaction with where you are headed. In doing so, you acknowledge that you have the power to adjust or modify your "ride." You can decide if you want to change where your life is headed.

QUESTIONS FOR EXPLORATION:

1. Describe the appearance of the rollercoaster. How does it relate to your current life situation or direction?

2. Is it a ride you would like to stay on for a while or get off of now?

3. Is the rollercoaster smooth or bumpy? Enjoyable or unenjoyable? Exciting or scary?

4. Is it a newer or older model? Does it appear sturdy?

5. How often is it inspected and cared for?

6. If you were riding it, would you be with someone or alone? How would you be feeling?

7. Has there ever been an accident related to it?

My Self-Representative House

PROCEDURE: Draw a house as if it actually embodied your personality, spirit, feelings, and thoughts. Think about its size, decoration, and shape. Consider whether it is simple or complex in design. Then, create an environment around it, such as a lush landscaped lot or city streets.

BENEFITS: It is beneficial to think about the way you view yourself, including how you choose to care for yourself and interact with others. This art project provides a non-threatening way to explore your own self-worth and self-image, including how you project these self-perceptions onto the world. It helps you consider whether you are isolating or welcoming people into your "home." Developing an awareness of how you care for yourself and interact with others is the first step toward change.

QUESTIONS FOR EXPLORATION:

1. Does the appearance of the house relate to your appearance? For example, is it plain or fancy? Overstated or understated? Gauche or tasteful?

2. Does it stand out, or is it lost in the background of the other houses?

3. Does it appear well-kept or is it in need of repair?

4. Did you include a variety of windows and doors, or is it missing them?

5. Does it appear welcoming or perhaps foreboding?

6. Is there smoke coming from the chimney? If so, what does that mean for you? For example, are you feeling angry or experiencing turmoil in your life?

7. Does the house contain everything an average house would have (e.g., windows, at least one door, a roof, a sidewalk or walkway leading to the front door)?

8. Who would you want to live in the house?

9. What would the neighborhood be like (e.g., quiet, busy, country, city-like)?

10. Is the house sturdy or fragile? For example, would it withstand a tornado?

Collage of Expectations and Hopes

PROCEDURE: Create a grouping of photos or drawings that symbolize your goals, desires, achievements, and events you anticipate will happen in the near and distant future. Examples may include finding a partner, having a baby, going to college, traveling, or feeling healthier.

BENEFITS: It is useful to focus on your desires and expectations so that you can create a plan of action toward achieving your goals. In addition, motivation is often enhanced once you are cognizant of your objectives and develop a timeframe to achieve them.

QUESTIONS FOR EXPLORATION:

1. Which pictures seem to be the most significant to you?

2. How many images do you view as realistic? How many are perhaps unrealistic?

3. Are there any parts of the collage that elicit strong feelings, such as joy or sadness?

4. Upon observation, do some of the photos surprise or motivate you in some way?

Color Wheel of Emotions

PROCEDURE: Using a paper plate, make an outline of a circle to create a pie chart with eight sections. Fill in each segment with drawings, magazine photos, colors, or images that represent an emotion. There should be one emotion per section. Think of emotions you tend to experience frequently, including happiness, sadness, frustration, anger, confusion, guilt, contempt, or mistrust.

BENEFITS: This exercise helps you become more aware of your emotions and how they affect your attitude, mood, motivation, and behaviors. You become empowered when you realize that your thoughts have a significant effect on the way you think, feel, and behave. Exploring and discussing emotions helps you become more comfortable with them.

QUESTIONS FOR EXPLORATION:

1. Which emotions are you currently feeling? How are they affecting your behavior and daily life?

2. Are there emotions included in your wheel that you are comfortable expressing? Which ones are you reluctant to express?

3. How do the images and colors that you incorporated into your wheel symbolize your present emotions and the feelings or behaviors they evoke?

The Figure and the Mountain Challenge

PROCEDURE: Draw yourself trying to get down a large, snowy mountain, like Mount Everest. Represent yourself any way you please, and think about ways you could descend the mountain (e.g., skiing, rolling, sledding, climbing down).

BENEFITS: This creative exercise provides an opportunity for you to metaphorically relate your current situation to the mountain, and to use your unique symbolism to explore how you handle life's obstacles.

QUESTIONS FOR EXPLORATION:

1. How are you attempting to get down the mountain? Are you rock climbing, skiing, snowboarding, or trying some other maneuver?

2. How are you feeling? Stressed or calm? Exhausted or energetic?

3. What is the weather like? Is it sunny and clear, foggy, or blizzard-like?

4. What's at the bottom of the mountain, and what's at the top?

5. What are the consequences if you don't get down the mountain?

6. Is there a timeframe to get to the bottom?

7. Do you want to get to the bottom, or for some reason do you want to stay where you are?

8. How would you describe the mountain? In your eyes, is it huge and insurmountable? Average-sized and doable? Rocky and full of sharp edges?

9. Do you view it as a healthy challenge or a torturous experience?

10. Is there anyone with you or are you alone?

Myself Inside Out

PROCEDURE: Create a drawing, collage, or sketch collage that represents what your inner self, spiritual self, and/or inner body looks like. As you create your design, think about how you would answer the question, "What is the essence of you?" For example, a drawing of a large heart may represent your kindness, a sketch of a large brain may symbolize intelligence, and a drawing of a bright light may signify that you are hopeful or religious.

BENEFITS: This exercise helps you develop awareness of who you really are (your authentic self), instead of focusing on the superficial aspects of yourself, such as how much money you earn, where you live, where you went to school, the color of your skin or hair, or your overall appearance. Much of the time, our essence isn't appreciated because we think we aren't meeting society's expectations of who we "should" be or how we should act at a certain age or stage in life. We confuse what is truly important in life, such as being a kindhearted and honest person, with fleeting, shallow standards that change with advertising and the politics of the day.

QUESTIONS FOR EXPLORATION:

1. What does your inner self look like? For instance, do you see beauty there?

2. Is your inner self different than your outer self? If so, in what ways?

3. Do you tend to judge yourself because of your appearance, finances, or the like?

4. Would taking the time to examine your authentic self help you accept various aspects of your personality, life, work, and relationships?

5. Did anything you drew about your inner self surprise you?

6. If your inner self looked like a person, what would their appearance be like? (See "Inner Self as a Figure" exercise.)

162

Inner Self as a Figure

PROCEDURE: Draw your essence ("your inner self") as a figure. The sketch should be totally focused on your feelings, spirituality, and your core – *not* on your normal outward appearance. Your inner self will dictate how you draw your outer self.

BENEFITS: This exercise helps you become cognizant of the importance of inner beauty, from which true strength and power is derived, as opposed to outer beauty, which is fleeting and superficial. You do not need to have a lot of money, be well schooled, or be free of illness or problems to have inner beauty. It is something that is "available for the wanting" and is necessary in order to have a productive and meaningful life.

QUESTIONS FOR EXPLORATION:

1. What is your meaning of beauty? Are there different types of beauty, and which type is most significant for you?

2. Is the figure you drew attractive or unattractive to you? Which part of the figure do you like the best?

3. What is your opinion of your inner self as depicted in the figure you created?

4. Do you believe there is a difference in attraction between your inner and outer self? Is this meaningful or inconsequential to you?

What Affects Me Today

PROCEDURE: Create a sketch or collage that answers the question, "What is affecting me today?" Include people, places, things, and emotions that have influenced the way you feel today. For example, you may have gotten into an argument with your friend earlier, spilled coffee in your car, ended up wearing different-colored socks, or been running on too little sleep, struggling with depression, or dealing with financial problems.

BENEFITS: Being aware of the way you react to daily occurrences, such as spilled coffee, will help you determine if you are comfortable with your behavior or wish to change how you perceive and handle encounters with others and your environment. This awareness gives you more control and stability in your life. It might protect you from negative thinking and unhealthy behaviors, such as road rage.

QUESTIONS FOR EXPLORATION:

1. What is affecting you most today? Is it something new, or has it affected you in the past?

2. How do you usually react to challenges that arise during the day?

3. Which item stands out most in your picture? Is it something important?

4. How would you ideally like to act when you encounter daily problems?

5. Who or what tends to "push your buttons"?

My Core Beliefs I

PROCEDURE: Take a piece of paper and fold it in half. On one side of the paper, draw some positive core beliefs you have about yourself, and on the other side, draw some negative core beliefs. Examples of core beliefs may include feeling you are intelligent or unintelligent, generally liked or disliked, a winner or a loser, lovable or unlovable, someone who always makes mistakes, or someone who is never good enough. You may also paint, add words and phrases, or use photos from magazines to illustrate your core beliefs; or you may choose to utilize colors, shapes, and forms to express your thoughts.

BENEFITS: Core beliefs are strongly held beliefs toward ourselves, others, and our environment. They are often deeply ingrained and frequently "owned" since childhood, and they affect our thoughts, feelings, behavior, motivation, and self-esteem. Self-awareness is the first step toward working through your negative core beliefs. In order to change them, you first need to become aware that they exist. Then, you can explore ways to transform them into more realistic thoughts, which gives you the freedom to think more positively. In turn, you can become more assertive and lead a more productive and meaningful life.

QUESTIONS FOR EXPLORATION:

1. How and when did your core beliefs form? Did they form during childhood, your teen years, or young adulthood? Did they emerge because of unfortunate experiences, or because of things other people said or did to you?

2. How do your core beliefs affect your self-worth?

3. Which core beliefs are your most positive? Which are your most negative?

4. Which core beliefs seem out of date and which ones hold true today?

5. How can you begin changing your undesirable core beliefs? What would be the first step toward transformation?

6. Is the positive side of your drawing stronger than the negative side or vice versa?

7. Is there evidence to support your current core beliefs?

8. How can you begin to focus on your strengths instead of your perceived weaknesses (e.g., engage in activities in which you excel, volunteer, socialize with positive people)?

My Core Beliefs II: Mandala Design

PROCEDURE: Using a paper plate, make an outline of a circle on a large piece of paper to form a mandala. Then, fill in the mandala with sketches, photos, words, images, and shapes that reflect both your positive and negative core beliefs. Examples of negative core beliefs may include, "I am a loser," "I can't do anything right," and "No one likes me," whereas examples of positive core beliefs may include, "I am smart," "I am creative," and "I am a likeable person."

BENEFITS: This mandala exercise helps you increase your understanding of your core beliefs and how they affect your self-esteem, motivation, relationships, and behavior. Exploring and clarifying your core beliefs is the first step toward understanding them, examining evidence regarding their validity, and ultimately changing them if they are harmful. When you reframe your negative core beliefs into positive ones, you are more likely to take care of yourself emotionally, physically, spiritually, and mentally.

QUESTIONS FOR EXPLORATION:

1. How did you represent your core beliefs in the mandala?

2. Does the mandala design appear optimistic, pessimistic, or somewhere in between?

3. Of the core beliefs you depicted, which ones are keeping you from fulfilling your goals?

4. Which ones are beneficial?

5. How would life be different for you if some of your beliefs changed?

6. How long have you had many of your beliefs?

7. What would happen if you allowed some of your negative beliefs to slowly dissipate? Which coping skills would you need to utilize in order for that to happen?

Circle of Life

PROCEDURE: Using a paper plate, make an outline of a circle to form a mandala. Fill in the circle with symbols that represent your own circle of life. Begin with images and figures representing your earliest memories (if you are comfortable doing so). Symbols may include awards or trophies, family members, memorable items of clothing (e.g., a cap and gown or wedding dress), hearts, stars, or people who have shaped you (e.g., close friends, partners, first love, parents, rabbi or priest, coach, teacher).

BENEFITS: Sharing various experiences and memories may enable you to better understand how you evolved into the person you are today. It can help you discover hidden strengths and resources, as well as the reasons for behavioral patterns and attitudes that help or hinder you in work, school, and relationships.

QUESTIONS FOR EXPLORATION:

1. Which past experiences have affected your attitude and outlook on life the most?

2. Have the changes in your life been easy, moderate, or difficult for you?

3. Where are you now in your unique circle of life?

4. If you could go back in time, is there anything you would change?

5. Which life stage would you like to revisit?

What I Am Keeping Locked Up

PROCEDURE: Draw a grouping of locks and then sketch, paint, or make a collage of things that you are keeping locked up (e.g., anger, fear, jealousy, guilt, sad memories, pain, rejection). *The participants may draw their own unique locks, or the group leader may provide sketch outlines of locks that participants can cut out, color in, and glue on the paper.*

BENEFITS: You gain increased control over your emotions and behavior when you develop self-awareness of that which you are hiding. When you realize the significance of the conflicts you are hiding, you can make informed decisions about whether it is healthy to keep these troubling thoughts, fears, and memories locked up, or if it is in your best interest to free them, analyze them, and eventually deal with them. When thoughts, feelings, and memories remained locked up in the recesses of our minds, symptoms such as headaches, gastrointestinal problems, and anxiety often emerge.

QUESTIONS FOR EXPLORATION:

1. How many locks did you include in your artwork? What do they look like?

2. Which locks seem easy to open and which appear foolproof?

3. Are there locks that need to remain locked, and are there locks that may be opened soon?

4. Which locks have been with you the longest? What purpose do they serve?

CLIENT RESPONSE:

A 34-year-old client named Barry tended to be evasive, moody and sarcastic, and generally isolated during group therapy. He was challenged with addiction issues and bipolar disorder. He shared, "I'd like a lock that I could open and close at will – personal freedom." He also said he locks himself out and doesn't interact with others because he has no personal identity. He said he doesn't know who he is. Art therapy gave him the opportunity to express his feelings in a non-threatening and accepting way; he felt comfortable enough to let his guard down for a brief while.

Calm and Chaotic Mind

PROCEDURE: Take a piece of paper and fold it in half. On one side of the page, draw your mind when it seems out of control, and on the other side, depict your peaceful, regulated mind.

BENEFITS: This exercise allows you to explore personal and environmental triggers that make you go into emotional mind, and it also allows you to examine ways to quiet the mind, such as music, meditation, and deep breathing. Drawing your feelings, experiences, and even your chaotic thoughts can help create a feeling of control and increased serenity.

QUESTIONS FOR EXPLORATION:

1. Which "mind" was easier to draw and which one did you draw first?

2. Which "mind" are you more comfortable experiencing?

3. Which "mind" do you tend to experience the most often?

4. When observing your artwork, which differences do you notice between the two pictures?

5. Which coping techniques seem to help you become better focused and peaceful?

The Art of My Life Canvas

PROCEDURE: Create a drawing depicting the colors, shapes, images, and overall feeling of your life as you currently experience it. For example, your work may be designed in shades of black and gray if you are presently feeling depressed, or your art may have a lot of disordered lines and movement if your thoughts are chaotic right now.

BENEFITS: Participating in this exercise helps you gain a greater understanding of your attitudes and thoughts about life. Exploring symbolic images and feelings depicted in your artwork helps you brainstorm ways to enhance contentment and draw upon your strengths and experiences to enhance your life canvas.

QUESTIONS FOR EXPLORATION:

1. How would you describe your current life canvas? Is it bright or dull? Full or empty?

2. What is the focal point of your artwork? Does it relate in any way to what is most important to you in life?

3. Would you like to change certain aspects of your life?

4. What in your life are you most satisfied with now?

5. Has your life canvas changed recently? Did you choose to change it?

6. What do you want to do with your canvas in the future? How would you like it to appear in terms of colors, movement, and shapes? How do you want it to reflect your thoughts, motivation, mood, health, relationships, etc.?

Lines of Emotion

PROCEDURE: Create a series of lines representing various emotions, making sure to emphasize the emotions that you experience most often. For example, you might draw a variety of wavy red lines to represent anxiety or zigzags to symbolize fear, which is an emotion that often stems from uncertainty. The following are examples of emotions that you can incorporate in your artwork:

- Anger
- Anxiety
- Contempt
- Disgust

- Excitement
- Fear
- Happiness
- Hope

- Sadness
- Surprise
- Shame

BENEFITS: This directive helps you gain a greater understanding of your emotional triggers and clarifies how emotions affect your mood, motivation, thoughts, and behavior.

QUESTIONS FOR EXPLORATION:

1. Which emotions were emphasized in your artwork?

2. How strong are the highlighted emotions?

3. How do those emotions affect your attitude and behavior?

4. Have your emotions ever kept you from engaging in a healthy activity or experience (e.g., applying for a job, asking someone out on a date, apologizing when you made a mistake)?

5. Do you tend to allow your emotions to rule you or are you in charge?

Doing What Works Right Now

PROCEDURE: Draw a picture illustrating what you need to do right now to improve your life. For example, you might need to apologize to a family member, change your job, say "no," move to a smaller home, or accept your current situation.

BENEFITS: This activity helps promote stress reduction, problem solving, greater motivation, and increased relief and contentment. It provides the opportunity for you to explore what needs to be done to work on goals and greater life satisfaction, while also allowing you to examine any roadblocks as well as your current attitude (e.g., is your attitude one of willingness or willfulness?). What might be standing in your way of a more fulfilled existence?

QUESTIONS FOR EXPLORATION:

1. What did you illustrate in your sketch? What do you need to do now to improve your current situation?

2. How can doing what works now relieve anxiety?

3. How does accepting your current situation affect your willingness to actively make the best of it?

Three Mountains of Life

PROCEDURE: Draw three separate mountains that represent your childhood, teenage years, and adult years, respectively. They don't have to be drawn in any specific order. Fill the mountains with words, symbols, images, and colors that represent your experiences in each of these time periods. As you create your mountains, think about your achievements, milestones, feelings, relationships, etc.

BENEFITS: By drawing the three mountains of your life, you develop increased self-awareness, self-compassion, and self-acceptance of the circumstances that have defined you. It also allows you to make more informed decisions regarding new goals and paths that you can create in the future.

QUESTIONS FOR EXPLORATION:

1. Are the mountains similar or dissimilar? If they are different, describe a few of the differences.

2. What are the most notable characteristics of each mountain?

3. Which mountain looks strongest? Which one appears most worn?

4. Which mountain would you like to climb or relax upon now? Which mountain, if any, would you avoid?

5. Upon which mountain have you had the best experiences? Worst experiences?

6. Which mountain looks like it will best stand up to environmental forces, like wind and snow?

Torn Paper Self-Portrait

PROCEDURE: Tear pieces of papers in varying sizes from construction paper and magazines. Work with the pieces to design a self-portrait that symbolizes you in some way (e.g., your traits, interests, appearance, relationships, experiences, moods). You may also add to the collage using markers, pastels, or paint if desired. In addition, you may choose to focus on just one aspect of yourself, such as your eyes or personality.

BENEFITS: Creating a unique self-portrait that focuses on the diverse aspects of yourself helps you answer the question, "Who am I?" It also enables you to more easily identify your goals, wants, and needs.

QUESTIONS FOR EXPLORATION:

1. Which parts of the portrait do you like most? The least?

2. How is your personality portrayed in your art?

3. Is there a part of the portrait that "speaks to you"?

4. How does your work represent your current self-esteem?

5. If you chose to speak to this self-portrait, what would you say to it (e.g., to yourself)?

CLIENT RESPONSE:

A 38-year-old man named Nate, who was experiencing depression and addiction issues, designed this self-portrait. He was very pleased with the outcome and asked the group leader to hang it in the art therapy room. The artwork represents his journey, starting from the throws of addiction leading up to his road to recovery.

Nate began his portrait on the left side of the paper where he wrote "Past" and then added a thin, pink semicircular shape piercing an orange wavy line, representing his road. The recovery road intersects a blue heart (his family), which leads to his home, "Home Sweet Home." To the left of the home is an orange circle symbolizing important goals, such as attending daily Alcoholics Anonymous meetings and being honest with his wife and other family members.

On the right-hand side, a red triangle represents changes that need to be made, such as being a strong, present father and a positive role model for his young children. The eyes symbolize him "finally waking up to the reality of my addiction, and the heartbreak I have caused because of it." The green rectangle on the bottom right side of the paper symbolizes "safety."

Nate remarked that he felt safe in the psychiatric program and, most importantly, safer within himself. He stated that he thinks he has gained more control over his actions and addictions, and that this increased control will help him cope and move forward.

Positive and Negative Thoughts

PROCEDURE: Draw the outline of a head and divide it in half. Fill in one side of the head with positive thoughts (e.g., "I am worthy," "I am smart") and the other side with negative thoughts you may be experiencing (e.g., "I am weak," "I will never reach my goals"). You may use magazine photos, words, designs, images, or color to represent these positive and negative thoughts.

BENEFITS: This exercise assists in increasing self-awareness, specifically in terms of how you view yourself and the ways in which your self-talk affects your mood, behavior, and self-esteem. Your emotions and behaviors are largely influenced by how you process your thoughts and the way you choose to think about yourself and your circumstances. Therefore, it is helpful to periodically examine and re-examine the messages you are sending and receiving, as we tend to believe what we repeatedly say to ourselves.

QUESTIONS FOR EXPLORATION:

1. Does your artwork depict more positive or negative thoughts?

2. How do the sides differ in artistic style and in reality?

3. Has your view of yourself changed recently? If so, what were some of the mitigating factors?

4. Does your mood, self-esteem, or behavior change when you focus on the positive?

5. What can you begin implementing today to begin focusing on brighter and more constructive thinking?

Tracking Changes with a Mood Graph

PROCEDURE: Draw a graph representing how your mood changes throughout the day.

BENEFITS: Increasing self-awareness of your daily mood patterns affords you an opportunity to better understand your thought patterns and environmental triggers. In turn, you can work with your moods to find the best time of day to focus on important goals, such as studying for exams, applying for a new job, or doing important errands and chores. You can use your graph to plan your daily schedule in a wise and structured manner so that you do what needs to be done when your energy is highest and you feel strongest.

QUESTIONS FOR EXPLORATION:

1. When is your mood brightest? Darkest?

2. Does your mood seem stable, or does it fluctuate a lot throughout the day?

3. What measures can you take to improve your mood when you feel depressed or anxious?

Self-Representative Animal

PROCEDURE: Draw an outline of an animal of your choosing, and then fill in the outline with images, designs, words, and phrases that demonstrate the ways in which the chosen animal relates to you. *The group leader may also provide outlines of a variety of animals for clients who desire more structure.* You can also incorporate doodle art into your animal design.

BENEFITS: This practice allows for exploration of one's wants and needs, and self-awareness of assets and capabilities. Choosing a distinct animal with specific characteristics may help you better understand your own needs, wants, and desires. For example, wanting to be a bird that flies may represent your desire to have more freedom in your life; or choosing a large lion with a full mane may represent a need to have more control.

QUESTIONS FOR EXPLORATION:

1. Which animal did you choose and why?

2. Which characteristics do you and the animal have in common?

3. How is the animal's life different from yours (e.g., its environment, relationships with other animals of the same species, amount of freedom, strengths and abilities)?

4. What characteristics and abilities do you admire most about this animal?

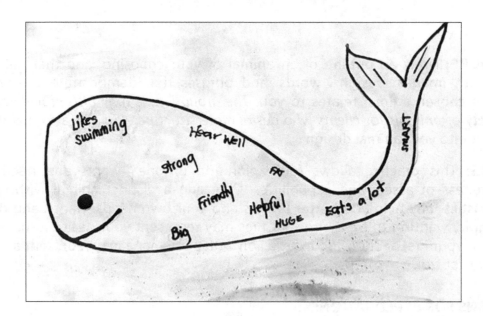

CLIENT RESPONSE:

A 42-year-old man named Steve related to the whale primarily because of its size and strength. Steve was obese and usually joked about his girth. He stated that as a human he is often teased and criticized, but as a whale he would be king. Steve remarked that he related to the whale because he loves swimming, especially freely swimming in the vast expanse of the ocean as opposed to the confinement of a pool.

He smiled as he light-heartedly bragged about his supersonic hearing, and his snoring, which "often sounds like a whale vocalization." He was able to share that whales are very smart, and that he excels in his knowledge of technology. He stated he is able to take apart and then put together a computer in a very short while. Steve acknowledged that he needed to focus on his positive qualities and be kinder to himself.

The Ostrich and Denial

PROCEDURE: Draw what you are in denial of or afraid or unwilling to deal with right now.

BENEFITS: Per an old myth, when ostriches feel that they are in danger, they bury their heads in the sand to hide from the potential threat. However, by burying their head, they make themselves more vulnerable to danger. Similarly, burying your head in the sand in response to difficult situations does not make the situation go away; it just prolongs the stress and delays the healing process. Hiding only keeps you stuck; you remain a victim and a prisoner of your circumstances. Instead, the first step toward change is to become aware of what needs changing. By acknowledging your problems and worries with this exercise, you can gain control and begin working on them in a slow but steady manner.

QUESTION FOR EXPLORATION:

1. What stands in the way of you accepting life as it really is?

2. How does denying your current situation help you?

3. What happens if you accept your current situation? How would you react physically and emotionally? Would your behavior change?

4. What coping skills can you use to accept reality?

Importance of Our Thoughts

"For there is nothing either good or bad, but thinking makes it so."
– William Shakespeare

PROCEDURE: With the Shakespeare quote in mind, draw the power of your thoughts using lines, shapes, and colors. Explore patterns, shading, and intensity of color. Think about positive and negative thoughts, logical and illogical thinking, and thoughts that become chaotic or muddled at times. Try to integrate all these thoughts into one cohesive design.

BENEFITS: This exercise helps you learn that you don't have to be controlled by your thoughts; you can choose to think differently much of the time. You have the choice whether or not to label people, places, experiences, and yourself as "good" or "bad." You have the ability to transform negative beliefs into more positive ones. Your thoughts don't define you. You can integrate both positive and negative thinking to create a colorful mixture that you can use to lead a productive life.

QUESTIONS FOR EXPLORATION:

1. How would you describe your artwork? For example, is it balanced? Do you notice patterns? Are there bold shapes and images included?

2. How does your picture relate to your general style of thinking?

3. Does the chaotic or illogical part of your artwork, as you view it, balance with the logical?

4. How can you integrate various aspects of your mood, attitude, and thinking so you can become more functional?

5. Do you acknowledge that you have the power to view things in your life differently right now? Do you *choose* to see things from a different perspective?

Positive and Negative Parts of My Life

PROCEDURE: Draw the positive aspects of your life on one side of the paper and the negative aspects of your life on the other side. You may include aspects of your life related to your relationships, health, milestones, losses, challenges, achievements, etc.

BENEFITS: This exercise provides a meaningful way for you to view your life from various perspectives and to understand that there will always be challenges. The goal is to work through the challenges instead of giving up, and to be mindful of the positive experiences that exist in spite of these challenges.

QUESTIONS FOR EXPLORATION:

1. How does acceptance play a role in overcoming obstacles?

2. Are you generally able to see "the bigger picture"?

3. Which side of the page was drawn first, and which side did you focus on more intensely?

4. Do you tend to dwell more on the positive or negative side of life?

5. Are you able to thoroughly enjoy festive events and beautiful moments in your life?

6. What is your responsibility in creating a worthwhile life?

7. How can you transform negative attitudes and thoughts into more positive ones?

Belief Balloons for Introspection

PROCEDURE: Draw a variety of balloons floating over a landscape and add symbols or words in the balloons that represent beliefs (positive and negative) you have about yourself, family, friends, your community, and the world. Sketch the landscape so that it represents your current mood in some way. For example, greenery with flowers might symbolize happiness, while a sparse landscape covered with clouds might represent a depressive mood.

BENEFITS: This exercise helps you to develop greater self-awareness regarding the beliefs that you have about yourself, others, and the world. When you maintain beliefs that are considered healthy (e.g., "Mistakes happen," "We are all unique"), this serves to improve life satisfaction and enhance self-esteem. In contrast, when you harbor a variety of negative beliefs (e.g., "I am a loser," "The world is a terrible place"), this can prevent you from living a happy and meaningful life. However, simply because you harbor these negative beliefs doesn't mean that they are true. You can examine the validity of these beliefs by asking others for their thoughts (e.g., "What's the evidence for and against this belief?") and by considering what you would tell a friend in the same situation. Doing so can help you challenge erroneous beliefs.

QUESTIONS FOR EXPLORATION:

1. Did you emphasize positive or negative beliefs?

2. Which beliefs tend to help you, and which ones tend to harm you?

3. Which beliefs would you like to keep, at least for now, and which ones would you like to see float away?

4. Has anyone disputed some of your unconstructive thoughts? If so, what was your reaction? Have you ever changed your viewpoints based on the reactions of others?

5. Is there any belief you need to change now? How would it help you if you changed it?

Shaky Ground Underfoot

PROCEDURE: Draw a picture of yourself standing on shaky ground, which is reflective of the situations in your life that elicit fear and uncertainty. You may literally draw a figure on shaky ground or use the term as a metaphor for stressful and anxiety-ridden experiences.

BENEFITS: The exercise helps you develop an awareness and better understanding of the effect that the environment has on your attitude, motivation, mood, and behavior. This enlightenment will help you develop a plan of action for dealing with uncomfortable situations.

QUESTIONS FOR EXPLORATION:

1. How unstable is the ground?

2. What is the ground composed of? For example, is it covered with concrete, mud, sand, stone, or grass?

3. Are you able to balance yourself?

4. How can you keep yourself steady?

5. What happens if you fall?

CLIENT RESPONSE:

George, a 54-year-old man recovering from alcohol and drug addiction, drew an eye-catching, frightening, skeletal-like figure with one foot on the ground and the other in the air, in a precarious position. The ground underneath the figure appears unsteady and "might be breaking away." As per George, the ground underneath him is falling apart; all he needs is a nudge and he will fall off the mountain into the depths below.

The figure is carrying a time piece in one hand (representing that he is almost out of time if he doesn't stop drinking and injecting heroin), and, in the other hand, he is carrying a hypodermic needle to symbolize his love of heroin and "all other drugs." The figure looks like death because "death is imminent if I don't change." George had two near-death experiences and his liver was deteriorating. George shared that he used bright colors to clothe the figure to represent some sort of hope and to make him appear somewhat comical "to take the edge off." George shared that he was thinking about getting a tattoo that looked like this figure to remind him to be clean and that he is in a very dangerous life-threatening situation.

Drawing My Story

PROCEDURE: Draw a chapter from your "story" ("story" meaning your life experiences), and illustrate it in any way you wish. You may choose to draw a significant experience, a particular period of time, such as your college or high school years, or a series of related events, such as dating, marriage, and then divorce.

BENEFITS: By drawing a chapter from your life story, you can come to the recognition that life is a process; there will be many chapters, and one chapter does not define your life or you as a person. Sharing your story helps connect you with others and enables you to gain a greater perspective as you retell the narrative of your life. Sharing can also be cathartic and places you in a position of control as the narrator and ultimately director of your life.

QUESTIONS FOR EXPLORATION:

1. How have the experiences you shared affected your life story and who you are today?

2. How would you rate your story so far? Would it get a 10%, 60%, or 100% rating on Rotten Tomatoes?[1]

3. What would you title your story so far?

4. Is there a hero in your story? A victim? A leading character?

5. What is the genre of your story thus far? Does it fall under the category of drama, comedy, satire, mystery, horror, or something else?

Leaving Our Comfort Zone

PROCEDURE: Using a paper plate, make an outline of a circle on a piece of paper. The inside of the circle will represent your comfort zone, the outline of your circle will be its perimeter, and the area outside of the circle will be considered new territory, which is out of your comfort zone. Fill in the circle with images that represent safety and comfort, and the outer area with images that make you feel uneasy, frightened, or anxious. The perimeter of the circle may be considered the "diving board" – the area where you balance yourself, contemplate what happens next, and get ready to make the "plunge" by taking healthy risks.

BENEFITS: This exercise helps you become more aware of behavioral and thinking patterns that may help or hinder your emotional and intellectual growth. It helps you understand that when you allow yourself to leave your comfort zone, even for a short while, you develop new skills and ideas, and you gain energy and strength. Growth, freedom, and self-esteem increase as you gain independence and take healthy risks.

QUESTIONS FOR EXPLORATION:

1. Did you tend to focus more on your comfort zone or the area surrounding it?

2. Which part of the drawing most closely represents the way you approach life?

3. Which images demonstrate trepidations you may have about leaving your comfort zone?

4. Which images show the adventurous side of your personality?

5. When was the last time you tried something new or stepped out of your comfort zone?

6. Do you tend to stay in your comfort zone, teeter on the border of it, or venture out of it, at least occasionally?

The Real Me

PROCEDURE: Draw your answer to the following statement: "If you really knew me, you'd…" Examples of artistic responses for consideration may include a large heart to represent a loving, warm person; an artist palette to symbolize someone who is creative; a face with tears to depict a sad individual; or a devil to represent someone who is mischievous or perhaps angry.

BENEFITS: This exercise helps enhance your awareness of how you present yourself to others versus how you view yourself. Occasionally, it is helpful to check in with others about these differences in self-perception because you may view yourself differently than the way other people view you. You certainly have the right to choose the way you perceive yourself, but you may be doing yourself a disservice, especially if you view yourself as unworthy or unlikeable while everyone else sees much value in your abilities and admires you.

QUESTIONS FOR EXPLORATION:

1. How did you introduce yourself, and which symbols or images reflect your spirit the most?

2. Do others tend to agree with the way you perceive yourself?

3. Are you helping yourself, misleading yourself, or hurting yourself with your self-analysis?

4. Do you present the "real you" to people in your life? If not, what are the reasons for staying guarded?

Middle of the Forest

PROCEDURE: Draw yourself walking through a forest. As you draw, think about the type of forest (e.g., bright and cheery, large and foreboding, full of treacherous pathways). In addition, consider how you will depict yourself. Are you tall and muscular, small and weak, confident or scared? Finally, ponder abstract questions such as "where, when, why, and how" in relation to your positioning in the forest.

BENEFITS: Participating in this exercise provides you an opportunity to explore your resourcefulness, problem-solving skills, and inner strength. Feelings about your current life path are examined and clarified. Present-day obstacles and problems may be examined, and pertinent coping skills assessed.

QUESTIONS FOR EXPLORATION:

1. How did you represent the forest? Is it lush, empty, welcoming, or foreboding?

2. Are there paths and other walkable areas, or is the forest filled with an overgrowth of grass, bushes, weeds, and trees?

3. Are there animals or other people in the woods, or are you alone?

4. Are you able to find your way out of the forest?

5. What is the temperature like? Are you warm, cold, or comfortable?

6. Are there obstacles in your way, such as large boulders, poison ivy, a family of skunks, or a snarling fox?

CLIENT RESPONSE:

Miles, a young man in his twenties, drew himself deep within the forest, sitting by a campfire roasting marshmallows. The fire is bright orange, and the flames are looming toward him to represent his overwhelming stress. He shared that he would like some time to be alone with nature and escape from his problems and his "annoying parents."

Miles mentioned that he is having trouble with his college classes because his concentration is poor, and he doesn't care about school. He feels very stressed, especially when his parents bother him to "get himself together" and graduate college. He said they don't understand depression and believe he is pretending to be ill to avoid his responsibilities. Miles stated he needs at least six months to unwind and stay away from family and other toxic people.

Symptoms as a Bubble

PROCEDURE: Draw your symptoms as they would look contained within a bubble. Examples of your symptoms may include crying, anxiety, stress, headaches, nightmares, moodiness, lack of energy, isolation, and overeating or undereating.

BENEFITS: Drawing your symptoms gives you an opportunity to examine how they affect various aspects of your life. In turn, you can determine if you are ready to learn methods to decrease them. This exercises also allows you to explore the "benefits" of having symptoms, which is a tongue-in-cheek way of exploring any payoffs derived from holding on to your stressors (e.g., receiving extra attention or not having to work as hard because others expect less of you).

QUESTIONS FOR EXPLORATION:

1. Is the bubble large or small? Is it strong or fragile?

2. Does the bubble appear stable, attached to the ground, or unsteady and about to float away?

3. Is there a way for the symptoms to escape from the bubble, or are they well contained?

4. What would happen if the bubble burst open?

A Cloud with Complex Emotions

PROCEDURE: Draw two clouds; one will be considered the outside of the cloud, and one will be considered the inside of the cloud. Design the outside of the cloud so that it appears positive – it may even include "a silver lining" – and then draw the inside of the cloud in a more complex manner so that it reflects both positive and negative colors, images, and feelings.

BENEFITS: Life is complicated, and it is helpful to understand that many of your experiences and relationships contain layers of complexity. For instance, "a cloud with a silver lining can still contain darkness and despair within it."[2] It is important to understand that we can be scared, sad, angry, and frustrated – but, at the same time, we can feel hopeful, loved, and motivated because we are complicated beings and are always thinking and experiencing life on many levels. There are so many ways to view yourself and life in general.

QUESTIONS FOR EXPLORATION:

1. How do the shapes, images, and colors of the cloud vary from the outside to the inside of the cloud?

2. Which part of the cloud dominates?

3. Is the cloud large or small? Still or in motion?

4. Is there anything stressful, dark, or scary in the cloud?

5. Do you think it is possible for a cloud to be decorated in bright silver but also hold darkness within it? Are you able to relate to this concept of being both happy and sad or frustrated at the same time?

Crocodile in My Vicinity

PROCEDURE: Draw yourself in relation to a crocodile. You may represent yourself as a person, stick figure, cartoon character, creature, or an amorphous shape. The crocodile may be situated next to you, far away, in a lake, on your bed, or somewhere else.

BENEFITS: This exercise helps you explore the sense of control and power that currently characterize your relationships, and it helps you develop an increased understanding of the things you may fear or need to conquer.

QUESTIONS FOR EXPLORATION:

1. Where in proximity to you is the crocodile?

2. How are you feeling in the picture?

3. What size and shape are both you and the crocodile?

4. Does the crocodile appear ominous or friendly? Apathetic or about to attack?

5. Who has the power in the picture?

6. Is there anyone in your life now or in the past who you can view as the crocodile?

7. Have you ever been the crocodile, or are you the crocodile now?

CLIENT RESPONSE:

Dan, a man in his twenties, drew himself in the jaws of the crocodile. He stated that he felt like he was trapped and wasn't sure how to escape. He complained that he disliked college and wasn't happy with his current relationship. He mentioned that his girlfriend, Chloe, was demanding and "acted like a stalker."

Dan felt like everyone he knew wanted him to act in a certain way, not allowing him to behave as he pleased. He particularly disliked that Chloe demanded that he stop smoking and insisted that he stop "hanging out" with his friends so often. He said he was considering taking a break from school and ending his year-long relationship with Chloe. He remarked that he wanted an apartment of his own and needed to get away from his parents, whom he characterized as ridiculously strict and overprotective.

Fog in the House

PROCEDURE: Draw a house that is filling up with a misty fog. You can decide how much fog there is, where it is located in the house, and how it affects the house. For example, is it weakening the structure of the house or is it creating a foul odor?

BENEFITS: Engaging in this exercise provides you an opportunity to explore how resourceful you are in handling any unknowns or uncertainties in life. It allows you to consider whether you give up easily, or whether you persevere even when there is fog blocking your view (e.g., when the way forward is unclear and difficult).

QUESTIONS FOR EXPLORATION:

1. Is the fog located in one area or is it spreading throughout the house?

2. Is the fog light or dark and thick?

3. To what degree does the fog block your sight?

4. How are you managing in the fog? How are you able to navigate throughout the house?

5. How does the fog symbolize any lack of clarity or obstacles you might have in your life?

Framing My Life

ADDITIONAL MATERIALS: Small stones, glitter, sequins, and other small collage materials.

PROCEDURE: Draw a frame, decorate it with tiny collage materials if desired, and then fill it in with a sketch of either your home, family, work life, memories, or the general way you currently view your life. You can use abstract designs to convey how you are feeling and thinking.

BENEFITS: This exercise allows you to assess your degree of life satisfaction and examine areas in your life that may need to be changed or improved upon. Developing a greater awareness of the various aspects of your life may also help you cultivate gratitude as you focus on people, places, and memories that are meaningful to you.

QUESTIONS FOR EXPLORATION:

1. Did you spend more time designing the frame or its contents?

2. Does the design of the frame relate to the pictures in it? For example, a brightly colored frame may be symbolic of a happy home life.

3. Who or what is included in the picture? How meaningful is the imagery drawn?

4. Is this frame something that you'd like to keep on a shelf in your home to remind you of what's currently occurring in your life and what is important to you?

Exploring the Journey of a Line

PROCEDURE: Create a personalized, self-representative line and take it on a journey over the entire sheet of paper. You may personalize the line by adding special symbols, colors, or designs. End the journey near an image or symbol that you find comforting, such as a house, park, welcoming friend, or pet.

BENEFITS: This exercise facilitates self-awareness by allowing you to gain a greater understanding of your goals, motivation, where you find comfort, and the way you are "moving along."

QUESTIONS FOR EXPLORATION:

1. In which ways do you relate to the line and its journey?

2. How is your life journey going now?

3. Are you following a smooth path or running into stumbling blocks?

4. Who or what seems to help you while traveling your road (e.g., friends, positive thinking, getting adequate sleep)?

5. Who or what may be getting in your way?

6. Has your road changed recently?

7. What do you like most about your road? Least?

8. What are your immediate goals?

Expressive Graffiti

PROCEDURE: Create a graffiti design that illustrates one or more of the following themes: your personality, thoughts, problems, attitudes, self-worth, family, likes/dislikes, fears, hopes/goals, anger, love/happiness. *An alternative exercise is to have participants design a graffiti mandala, which provides a little more structure.*

BENEFITS: This creative exercise provides a healthy outlet to share your emotions, thoughts, and concerns. In doing so, you gain greater self-awareness regarding your identity, values, and purpose. By expressing yourself with graffiti, you can also create a "shout-out" to various people in your life and society in general. You may feel in control as you examine and express your wants, needs, and feelings.

QUESTIONS FOR EXPLORATION:

1. In which ways are your personality traits and your views represented in your graffiti?

2. Which messages did you try to convey?

3. Does designing graffiti make you feel more in control or out of control?

4. Were you able to allow yourself to have fun with the art form, or was it difficult to allow your art to flow?

Running a Life Race

PROCEDURE: Create a figure running in a race. You can decide what type of race you are running (e.g., the New York Marathon, Race for a Cure®), as well as what the environment is like surrounding the race course (e.g., other racers, a group of onlookers cheering, a wooded forest, a sky full of clouds, a sun shining upon a field of lovely green foliage).

BENEFITS: Life can be compared to a race (e.g., a "rat race"). Although a rat race has a negative connotation, developing an awareness of your own lifestyle helps you develop greater insight into the type of race you are engaging in now. Opening your eyes regarding your role in your own personal marathon allows you to slow down, pace yourself, become more aware of your surroundings, and take the time to be mindful and maintain a steady pace.

QUESTIONS FOR EXPLORATION:

1. What type of race is the figure running?

2. Is the figure at the beginning, middle, or end of the race?

3. Where is the figure in comparison to the other participants?

4. How fast is the figure running?

5. What is the reward for running in the race? For winning the race?

6. Is it important to win the race?

7. What happens if the figure loses the race?

8. Where is the location of the race?

9. Are you able to relate to the figure in regard to where you are in your life right now? For example, are you just beginning to form relationships, or are you first starting in the work world? Are you where you "should" be in life? Do you compare yourself to others?

chapter six

self-esteem & self-acceptance

Self-esteem is a reflection of our overall sense of self-worth, both in terms of how we value ourselves and how valuable we believe we are to others and the world.[1] According to Nathaniel Branden, Ph.D., a psychotherapist and expert on self-esteem, self-esteem is "the experience of being competent to cope with the basic challenges of life and of being worthy of happiness."[2] Self-esteem develops from many sources, including our self-appraisal, achievements, parental evaluation, acceptance by friends and significant people in our lives, and the challenges we have faced throughout the years.

Although many people base their self-worth on external factors (e.g., profession, physical appearance, partner or lack thereof, wealth), doing so can be tenuous, as these factors can change with time. For example, if you base your self-esteem on how much money you make, then you are likely to feel vulnerable and defeated if you get demoted or lose your job. On the other hand, basing your self-worth on your unique qualities and strengths provides a deeper and more valuable source of satisfaction. It will stand the test of time. You feel worthwhile because you recognize that you are just a human being doing your best to get by in the world. Instead of feeling permanently defeated when you experience loss or failure, you bounce back quicker and begin anew. You understand that failing does not make you a failure, and that success comes from the ability to get back up and try again.

Self-esteem is closely related to the notion of self-acceptance, though the two terms vary slightly. Self-esteem is an indicator of how worthy or valuable we see ourselves as a person, whereas self-acceptance involves accepting ourselves *as we are* even in light of our failures, problems, and flaws. It requires accepting everything about ourselves, as opposed to just the more worthy, "esteem-able" parts.[3] Therefore, self-acceptance is one of the pillars of self-esteem, as feeling worthy requires that we first unconditionally accept ourselves for who we are.

Self-esteem and self-acceptance are the building blocks of wellness. They help us rebound from failure and loss more quickly, and they give us the impetus to fight and struggle for a better existence. As children, we have less power to change our circumstances, but as adults we can work toward developing greater self-awareness of our behaviors and changing negative thought patterns that interfere with our sense of self-worth. Our thinking plays a huge role in the decisions we make regarding who we are and what type of person we'd like to become in the future. In essence, we define ourselves.

The exercises in this chapter are intended to enhance feelings of self-acceptance and self-esteem. They are meant to help individuals accept themselves for who they are and put energy into creating goals instead of letting self-defeating thoughts and behaviors get in the way. Each exercise tackles this subject in a different but meaningful manner. The more techniques that people have at their fingertips to enhance their feelings of worthiness, the stronger and more in control they will be.

My Personal Power

PROCEDURE: Draw the power you have now. Think about the physical and emotional capabilities, strengths, and abilities you possess in this moment. Examples may include the ability to forgive, to stop engaging in negative self-talk, to make amends, to volunteer, to make someone feel more comfortable, to teach others, to change your attitude, to clean your house, or to stop engaging in unhealthy behaviors (e.g., overeating, smoking).

BENEFITS: You are often stronger than you think; therefore, it is helpful to explore your strengths so you can acknowledge them, own them, and then utilize them to help you cope and move forward.

QUESTIONS FOR EXPLORATION:

1. What do you perceive to be your most important power?

2. Are you acknowledging your power(s) and are you using it wisely?

3. Did you include any strengths you had previously been unaware of or ignored?

4. How have your powers served you in the past, and how can they help you in the present and future?

5. If you could possess any power (real or imaginary), what power would you want to have?

6. Who is the most powerful person you know now or have known in the past?

Glitter and Shine Mandala

ADDITIONAL MATERIALS: Sequins, glitter, glue (e.g., Elmer's® or Aleene's® glue work well), colored stones, and small, shiny beads or other similar objects.

PROCEDURE: Using a paper plate, make an outline of a circle to form a mandala. Then, fill it with different colored glitter, sequins, shimmering stones, and any other shiny objects. You can also use glittery pens and markers to create your design.

BENEFITS: Creating this mandala allows you to examine the various ways that you shine and stand out in life. It gives you a chance to explore and share your strengths and talents. It is important to discover and reinforce the types of things that put a twinkle in your eyes.

QUESTIONS FOR EXPLORATION:

1. What type of people, places, feelings, or experiences make you feel joyful and fulfilled?

2. When was the last time you felt like you were glistening?

3. How can you engage in more pleasurable experiences and enhance the positive feelings you have toward yourself and others?

Crown of Uniqueness

PROCEDURE: Draw, paint, sculpt, or create a collage of your own unique crown. Your crown might represent your abilities, talents, achievements, strengths, roles in life, or privileges you have earned over the years.

BENEFITS: The exercise helps you appreciate and acknowledge your positive traits and achievements. The crown becomes a symbolic representation of self-worth and your unique characteristics and strengths. It helps us realize that perhaps we are all worthy of wearing a symbolic crown.

QUESTIONS FOR EXPLORATION:

1. What is special about this crown?

2. Do you believe you deserve to wear it?

3. How often do you wear it?

4. Has it been worn before?

5. What does it look like? Is it simple or ornate? Light or heavy?

6. Are there benefits or problems associated with wearing the crown?

7. Is this crown something you will share, or will it be worn solely by you?

Exploring Body Image

PROCEDURE: Draw the outline of a person that covers most of the page. *The group leader can also distribute an outline of the human form to those who desire more structure.* Then, fill in the figure with thoughts about your body, such as whether you find it to be strong, weak, healthy, sick, adaptable, athletic, or attractive. As you fill in the figure, consider what your body does for you on a daily basis (e.g., allows you to walk, run, dance, hug, heal, live, work). In addition, you may add anything to the figure that represents you in some way, including your desires, personality traits, likes, dislikes, problems, achievements, memories, affirmations, or people who are important to you. Finally, you can add any thoughts, comments, images, sketches, or doodles to the area surrounding the figure.

BENEFITS: Our body image often affects how we interact with others and our motivation to take care of ourselves. This exercise helps you develop a greater understanding of how your attitudes and thoughts about your body affect your self-image and self-esteem. It helps you recognize that it is important to focus on the way your body helps you and that you have to take care of your body in order for it to function effectively. Most importantly, when you learn that your inner self is key, you can better accept your outward appearance and understand your true beauty and uniqueness.

QUESTIONS FOR EXPLORATION:

1. What is your reaction to the body you designed?

2. Which part of the body is most pleasing? Least pleasing?

3. Where is the beauty in your picture?

4. Has your body changed in recent years?

5. Is there anything you would like to change in your artwork?

6. When has your body "come through" for you?

7. When has it been a challenge?

8. What would you like to ask or say to your body? You may speak to your artwork.

9. How does your body image affect your self-esteem?

10. What can you do to "feed" your body and soul?

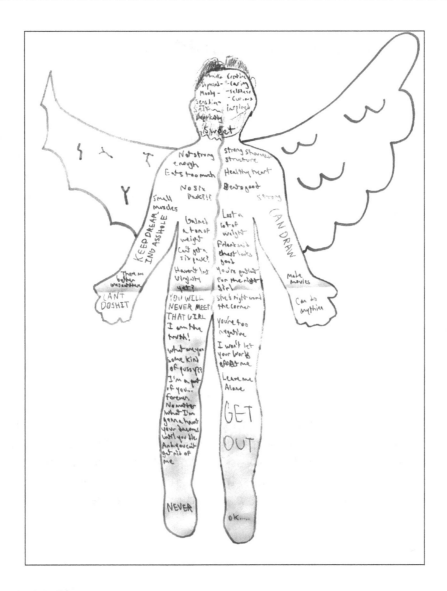

CLIENT RESPONSE:

Travis, a 20-year-old man with bipolar disorder, designed this figure with angel wings. The figure is divided in half by a light green wavy line. One side of the body contains negative statements, which are refuted by positive statements on the other side of the body. A few examples include: "Not strong enough "versus" strong shoulder," "You're too negative "versus" I am the truth," and "Leave me alone "versus" I'm a part of you forever."

The angel wings are also divided; the right side symbolizes flight and freedom, and the left side represents weakness and disability. Travis shared that the wings represent his wish to fly and his desire for others to be happy even when he is depressed. He remarked that his mother used to refer to him as an angel when he was a little boy. He said he never understood why she said that because he never felt angelic or worthy. Travis shared that he is constantly trying to control his thoughts and think more positively, but it is an exhausting and ongoing struggle.

Affirmation Shape Design

PROCEDURE: Create a large shape on the paper and fill it in with positive affirmations, photos, and sketches that lift your mood and spirit. *The group leader can also provide participants with a handout containing a variety of affirmations that they can copy or glue onto their design.* The shape may be round, square, or triangular, or it can be an amorphous shape that takes form as you freely move your pencil or marker. Add colors, designs, and images to complete your artwork. The following are some examples of positive affirmations that you could include in your design:

- "I am worthy."

- "I am deserving of love."

- "I am enough."

- "I attract positive people."

- "I can do what I need to do to accomplish my goals."

BENEFITS: Positive affirmations can help you reprogram your thinking patterns and reduce negative thinking and self-defeating behavior.[4] Reciting these affirmations on a regular basis can remind you to take advantage of life's possibilities and train you to follow your dreams and pursue goals. In turn, it increases motivation and positive self-esteem. Ideally, this artwork should be hung on a refrigerator or wall where it can be viewed periodically for inspiration.

QUESTIONS FOR EXPLORATION:

1. How does your artwork reflect your attitude and self-worth? Does it symbolize changes that need to be made in your overall outlook?

2. How does your design represent your thoughts and aspirations?

3. Which affirmations did you find the most helpful?

4. Which affirmations will you begin using today to help encourage you to move forward?

Power Mask I

ADDITIONAL MATERIALS: Cut-out cardboard masks and collage materials, such as sequins, pom-poms, and glitter.

PROCEDURE: Use a ready-made cardboard or papier-mâché mask, or design your own from scratch, and transform it into a mask suitable for a superhero. Add personal images, colors, and collage materials to represent "the superhero within." Decorate the mask by representing areas in which you excel and achievements for which you feel proud. For example, you may be proud for being a dedicated caregiver to the elderly, a devoted parent, someone who is steadily working toward better health, someone who was able to overcome an addiction, or someone who survived a traumatic experience. Sometimes, just surviving day-to-day may be considered heroic. You may also depict yourself as a known superhero, like Superman®, Wonder Woman®, Wolverine®, Iron Man®, or Batman®.

BENEFITS: Everyone has their own definition of power and what it means to be a superhero. Some people may view a superhero as someone who excels at sports or someone who saves other people from danger, like a firefighter, military personnel, or police officer. Others view a superhero as someone who has a kind heart and who is generous and giving, such as a person who donates a kidney to another individual in need. Many young children view their parents as superheroes because of their warm, loving manner and undeniable love. People who persevere through trying times can also be considered superheroes.

QUESTIONS FOR EXPLORATION:

1. What type of superhero did you represent? What super qualities do you possess?

2. Which specific strengths are symbolized in the design of your mask?

3. Which known superheroes do you admire?

4. Are you able to relate to any of the superheroes in terms of personality characteristics, behavior, or strengths?

5. Which special power do you wish you could possess? How would it enhance your well-being?

6. How can you nurture your current capabilities?

Power Mask II

ADDITIONAL MATERIALS: Cut-out cardboard masks and collage materials, such as sequins, pom-poms, and glitter.

PROCEDURE: Design a mask that represents a fantasy power (or powers) that you would like to possess. Examples of powers may include the ability to fly, to have superhuman strength, to read people's minds, and to become invisible.

BENEFITS: Exploring the imaginary strengths you would like to have can help you realize your own value and potential. While you may not possess fantasy attributes like x-ray vision, you can refine your own powers – like mindfulness and thoughtfulness – to increase your sensitivity to others and your surroundings, and to become more cognizant of your wants and needs and the needs of others. This exercise helps you learn that you can make the most of the strengths you do possess and be powerful in your own unique way.

QUESTIONS FOR EXPLORATION:

1. Which powers are represented by your mask?

2. What would you do with the powers you selected, and how might your life be different if you possessed those strengths?

3. Does viewing this mask seem to inspire or benefit you in any way?

4. How are you reflected in the mask (e.g., in terms of its appearance, design, meaning)?

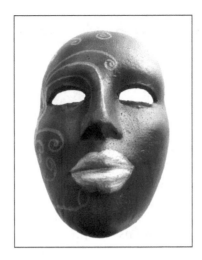

CLIENT RESPONSE:

A 30-year-old woman named Bridget, who was dealing with legal issues and about to get evicted from her apartment, designed this mask in about 20 minutes. She painted a quick layer of black tempera on the cardboard base, placed it on a sunny ledge to dry, and then used glittery permanent marker to create the swirly face design.

Bridget shared that the mask's power lies in its ability to acquire large sums of money in a blink of the eye. She remarked that whoever wore the mask and saw someone in need would immediately be able to conjure up thousands of dollars to give to that unfortunate person. Bridget laughed and shared that she would be the first one the mask would help since lack of finances was one of her major issues. She believed if she had enough money for her needs that her stress level would lessen, and she could function more effectively.

During discussion, Bridget did say she that she was able to relate to the mask in that she also viewed herself as beautiful and strong, and she had been successful in the past until addiction destroyed much of her life.

She lost her family, her job, a large, beautiful house, and much of her dignity. In an annoyed manner, she stated that anyone who says money doesn't matter was never poor.

Dominance of the Warrior

PROCEDURE: Think about the traits that embody a warrior. For example, they are strong, determined, skillful, loyal, brave, and disciplined. They rise to challenges, try to right wrongs, and take healthy risks. A warrior "gets back on the horse" when they fall. Next, draw yourself as a warrior in any way you please. You can use forms, figures, or draw the feeling you would experience as a warrior.

BENEFITS: This exercise helps you explore your strengths and skills, including the ways in which you handle obstacles in life. It allows you to gain new insights regarding how it feels to be a warrior versus someone who takes a passive role in life. Developing this awareness is a very important trait of the "spiritual warrior."

QUESTIONS FOR EXPLORATION:

1. How do you relate to the figure drawn?

2. Which positive qualities are you able to identify with, and which characteristics do you view as assets?

3. Currently, do you view yourself more as a warrior, average person, passive person, or victim?

4. How can you become more like a warrior in the future? Which skills would you need to develop?

Low Self-Esteem Garbage Can

ADDITIONAL MATERIALS: Scissors and a bucket or garbage can.

PROCEDURE: Draw an image representing what low self-esteem might look like as a piece of art. Think about the size, shape, colors, and feelings associated with it. Then, cut the representation out and decide whether you want to keep your "low self-esteem" or throw it out into a bucket in the middle of the room. If you decide to throw it out, say something positive about yourself or your life before discarding the representation into the bucket.

BENEFITS: This exercise gives you the opportunity to explore and examine your low self-worth by drawing it and then assessing what to do with it symbolically. Participating in this exercise helps create a greater awareness of negative attitudes and behavioral patterns that do not serve you (e.g., "Why would someone hold on to their low self-esteem? Where did it come from and how long have they had it?"). It allows you to explore the importance of taking responsibility for your attitudes and life direction.

QUESTIONS FOR EXPLORATION:

1. What did your drawing look like, and what was your reaction to it?

2. Did you choose to keep the low self-esteem symbol or throw it out?

3. How do you believe your self-esteem was formed (e.g., your parents, friends, abilities, life experiences, negative self-talk)?

4. Which positive traits are you most proud of and which personality characteristics need continued development?

Inner Strength Mandala

PROCEDURE: Using a paper plate, make an outline of a circle to form a mandala. Then, draw your inner strength within the circle. Think about the size, shape, color, and force of your inner strength. You can also add words and images to the mandala.

BENEFITS: By creating a work of art that symbolizes your inner strength, you can recognize all your positive characteristics that have been unacknowledged or disregarded, and you can increase feelings of self-worth and confidence.

QUESTIONS FOR EXPLORATION:

1. What are your reactions to your mandala?

2. Does it reflect your inner strength?

3. What do the size, colors, and shapes represent?

4. Has your inner strength always been the same throughout the years?

5. When did you feel the strongest?

6. What gives you strength?

7. What depletes it?

8. Do you have the amount of strength you would ideally like to have?

9. How did you feel while you were drawing? Was the exercise easy, moderate, or difficult?

10. If you could change the drawing (your degree of strength), would you?

Coping Mug

ADDITIONAL MATERIALS: Cup or mug, large popsicle sticks or tongue depressors.

PROCEDURE: Write a variety of positive affirmations, words, and coping skills on popsicle sticks, and then decorate them if desired. When you are finished, place the sticks in a plain mug or cup. You may decorate the mug using decoupage, permanent markers, or glass paint. Eventually, you will have a mug filled with affirmations that you can peruse when the mood strikes. You may even give the affirmations to friends and family members to lift their spirits and provide extra motivation.

BENEFITS: This coping mug becomes a go-to support item you can use when you are feeling stressed or unworthy. You can choose to review one or more of the popsicle sticks whenever you need some inspiration or need to be reminded of your strengths.

QUESTIONS FOR EXPLORATION:

1. Which affirmations tend to increase your confidence and motivation?

2. When was the last time you used positive words and phrases to comfort yourself or help you feel more self-assured?

3. Do you have other systems in place to help you cope when you need an extra boost to improve your mood or self-esteem?

Drawing on Strengths

PROCEDURE: Fold a piece of paper in half, and on the bottom half of your paper, represent your strengths using images, lines, shapes, and designs. You may also add words and phrases for further clarification. Then, use the top half of the paper to draw any problems, concerns, or stressors in your life. When finished, examine how the strengths you have listed can help you deal with these stressors.

BENEFITS: This exercise encourages you to notice the connection between your strengths and the conflicts that are represented. You may begin to see that you possess the capabilities and resources to deal with many life issues and concerns that may seem insurmountable right now.

QUESTIONS FOR EXPLORATION:

1. How does your artwork symbolize the way you approach life's problems?

2. Do you utilize all of your inner resources to deal with difficulties?

3. Which of your strengths are you most proud of and which ones seem to be the most helpful?

4. How can you use your abilities to help you overcome some of your most pressing problems?

Assertiveness for Self-Respect

PROCEDURE: Using a paper plate as a template, draw two large circles overlapping. In the circle on the left, draw symbols of ways in which you act or have acted in an aggressive manner. In the circle on the right, draw ways in which you have acted passively. In the middle, the region where the circles overlap, draw ways in which you have engaged in assertive behavior. You may add words and phrases to your design, and you can use magazine photos if desired as well.

TERMS

- **Passive:** Do not stand up for your needs or rights, act obedient or subdued, have difficulty saying "no."

- **Assertive:** Are strong but calm when speaking up for yourself, do not allow others to direct your behavior, authoritative, confidently exercise your rights but do not deny the rights of others.

- **Aggressive:** Engage in threatening or physical behavior that intimidates others, act in an aggressive or belligerent manner, are combative or forceful.

BENEFITS: You can develop increased self-awareness and self-respect by learning and implementing effective assertiveness and communication techniques. Examining the difference between assertive, passive, and aggressive behavior helps you examine the most effective ways to get your needs met. In turn, you can improve your sense of control and increase self-esteem in your daily interactions.

QUESTIONS FOR EXPLORATION:

1. Which of the three communication techniques do you tend to engage in the most? In which ways do you find the techniques effective or ineffective?

2. When was the last time you acted assertively? How did it feel? Did you get your needs met?

3. Which part of the design did you find easiest to fill in and which part was most difficult?

4. Which circle seems to be your focus? Which circle is the fullest? Which one is most meaningful?

Empowering Myself

PROCEDURE: In the center of the paper, draw a figure, shape, or other image that symbolizes you in some way. Then, surround it with ways to make yourself stronger, motivated, happier, less stressed, and more confident. You may also surround the central figure with positive traits and goals.

BENEFITS: Completing this exercise helps you to focus on the different ways in which you can empower yourself. It helps you develop a greater awareness of your abilities and talents, and it awakens you to your unique powers, especially during a period of time when you may feel powerless.

QUESTIONS FOR EXPLORATION:

1. How is this artwork inspiring?

2. In which ways does the central figure symbolize you?

3. What seems to be the connection between the central figure and the positive symbols surrounding it? For example, is the figure close to the symbols or distant? Does the figure seem to be an entity unto itself or is it reaching outwards?

4. What sources of empowerment will help you the most right now?

5. Are you able to acknowledge your strengths?

6. How does self-acceptance play a role in feeling empowered?

Moving Forward with Tiny Victories

PROCEDURE: Fold your paper in fourths and fill in each section with small achievements. Examples may include learning to cook or sew, getting a driver's license, learning to swim or ride a bicycle, socializing even though you are hesitant to approach people, going to the supermarket when you fear crowds, or learning a new coping technique to help decrease anxiety.

BENEFITS: Engaging in this artistic prompt helps you understand the importance of taking healthy risks, as well as the positive impact that these risks have on your self-esteem and motivation. This exercise provides you with the opportunity to focus on your strengths and helps you realize that small successes are significant. Even tiny victories can move you toward success and happiness.

QUESTIONS FOR EXPLORATION:

1. Which victory do you value the most?

2. Are you able to praise yourself for your achievement?

3. Which healthy risk are you contemplating taking soon or in the distant future? What, if any, barriers are stopping you from acting sooner rather than later?

4. How does taking small steps toward success help with motivation and stress reduction?

Road of Acceptance

PROCEDURE: Draw a personalized road and fill it with all the things that you need to accept in order to reduce stress, feel happier, and move on with your life. For example, you may need to accept a loss or move, a lifestyle or attitude you disapprove of from your adult children, being fired from a job, getting a divorce, aging, illness, or not achieving your goals. As you create your drawing, think about the size, shape, length, and sturdiness of the road.

BENEFITS: Accepting yourself and your life situation plays a large part in reducing stress and enhancing self-esteem. When you practice acceptance, it doesn't mean that you don't work toward self-improvement or desired goals. Rather, it means acknowledging that certain circumstances, traits, and experiences cannot be changed. Doing so allows you to focus on that which is in your control instead of what is out of your control, which can help you feel more at peace. Acceptance helps you tolerate distressing situations and enables you to move on while tolerating the moment.

QUESTIONS FOR EXPLORATION:

1. What does your road look like? Is it flat or bumpy? Long or short? Winding or rigid?

2. Are there obstacles on your road? How can you deal with them?

3. What do you need to accept? How are the things you need to accept symbolized on your road?

4. Are there many, moderate, or few things to accept? Is acceptance doable for you? Can you begin now, soon, or do you need to wait awhile?

5. Do you have a support system to help you make needed changes?

6. What strengths do you possess that will help you continue down your life path regardless of issues and problems that may arise or are planted firmly on the road?

CLIENT RESPONSE:

Mark, a 57-year-old man with a lifetime of addiction issues, drew a "very bad" road. Mark shared he had "done a lot of shit" in his life, but he was trying to make life better now for his wife, children, and himself. A diagnosis of liver cancer woke him up to the devastating effects his drinking had on all aspects of his life. The cancer diagnosis was the first thing he ever experienced that really scared him. He was terrified of being ignored by his family and dying alone.

A bottle of whiskey is the first item on his road, and it is drawn with a skull and crossbones to signify its deadly effects on Mark's body and soul. The car represents a recent accident where he hit a pedestrian walking in a crosswalk while he was driving under the influence of alcohol. The pedestrian broke his arm and had a minor concussion, but miraculously didn't suffer any major injuries. The next item is a broken heart representing the many times Mark disappointed and hurt both his wife and children. His children are situated on the road to represent his neglect of them over the years, including missing a number of birthday parties, school plays, holidays, and baseball games due to being drunk and "out of it." He said that he would spend the rest of his life trying to make amends for all of this disregard and mistreatment of his family.

Yes, You Can

PROCEDURE: Write the words "You can" on the left-hand side of the page, and place an arrow pointing toward the right, directly under the phrase. To the right of the arrow, add drawings of things that you are able to do, want to do, and believe you will accomplish in the near and distant future. Examples may include having a relationship, graduating from school, changing jobs, etc.

BENEFITS: This exercise promotes encouragement, motivation, self-awareness, and exploration of strengths and goals. This exercise helps you examine goals and methods to attain the goals, while acknowledging and celebrating your capabilities, coping skills, talents and overall self-worth.

QUESTIONS FOR EXPLORATION:

1. What is the significance of the images you added to the overall picture?

2. Were you surprised by any of the illustrations added?

3. Were any significant hopes, desires, or goals added or left out of the picture?

4. Is the pointed arrow meaningful in any way? For example, a large, bright arrow might signify strong positive feelings.

5. Which sketch symbolizes your current focus?

6. Do you ever doubt your abilities?

7. What is one thing you can do today to begin your journey toward wellness and productivity?

Self-Esteem Changes Through Time

ADDITIONAL MATERIALS: Easy-to-manipulate clay that can air dry (e.g., Crayola® Model Magic or Air-Dry Clay), modeling tools if available.

PROCEDURE: Take the clay and mold it into at least four or more shapes that represent your self-esteem. Then, place the shapes in chronological order to reflect the changes in your self-esteem over the years.

BENEFITS: Engaging in this exercise helps you explore and understand the internal and external building blocks of your self-esteem. By exploring changes in your self-esteem across time, you can become cognizant of the ways in which outside forces affect your dignity and motivation to achieve your goals. It helps you realize what experiences, relationships, and accomplishments have positively impacted your self-worth, as well as what experiences have acted as barriers.

QUESTIONS FOR EXPLORATION:

1. What changes do you notice in the sculptures?

2. Are the changes mild, moderate, or significant?

3. Where do you notice the most change?

4. What does the arrangement of the figures say about your experiences and resulting feelings of self-worth or lack thereof?

Myself in Perspective

ADDITIONAL MATERIALS: A 6 × 4 inch box. (An empty Keurig® coffee box that contained 12 pods works.)

PROCEDURE: *Before beginning the exercise, the group leader will briefly discuss the idea that everyone is unique and has many different personality characteristics.* Represent various aspects of your personality, thoughts, and feelings on each side of the box. For instance, one side of the box may include your strengths, another side may represent your goals, and another may symbolize your worries and fears. Or, one side may represent the outgoing side of your personality and another may represent your quiet, introspective side. The following are some examples of themes that can be included on each side of the box *(if need be, a list of personality traits can be provided for further clarification)*:

- Worries and fears

- Affirmations and positive thoughts

- Strengths

- What you have to work on to feel more in control

- What you hide

- What you show to the world

- Goals

- Dreams and desires

- How you think others see you

- How you see yourself

- Hobbies and interests

- Beliefs

- Achievements

- Your wisdom

BENEFITS: Engaging in this project provides you with new perspectives regarding your strengths, goals, and personality traits. Developing an awareness that you are multifaced is affirming and enlightening, and it increases self-esteem. You don't want to "box yourself" into a label (e.g., an addict, bipolar, unintelligent, a loser, unworthy) because, as humans, we are so complex.

QUESTIONS FOR EXPLORATION:

1. How does your box represent various aspects of your personality?

2. Which side of the box is your favorite? Which side is your least favorite?

3. Did any sketches or symbols placed on the box surprise you? Did you add aspects of your personality to the box that you hadn't thought of or explored recently?

4. Did you tend to stick with just one side of the box (e.g., the worries/fears side or the hopes/dreams side)?

5. What messages does the box design provide for you?

6. How can you continue to remember that you are complex and have much to contribute to others (e.g., recite positive affirmations, help others, keep learning, stay positive)?

My Inner Fantasy Character

PROCEDURE: Draw yourself as a fantasy character, such as an elf, wizard, fairy, king, or queen. The characters you sketch may possess whatever traits(s) you wish, but some characteristics to think about may include physical power, emotional strength, tenacity, agility, leadership, and courage.

BENEFITS: Exploring positive characteristics of the character you chose may help you continue to develop similar strengths that will help you feel motivated and increase self-esteem. You can cultivate your own strengths by drawing on this inner fantasy character.

QUESTIONS FOR EXPLORATION:

1. In which ways is the character similar to you? Dissimilar to you?

2. What about the character is attractive to you?

3. What are the reasons you chose to create this character?

4. Would you like to be like this figure?

5. How would your life be different if you were to be more like this figure?

chapter seven
self-care

Self-care involves taking deliberate actions to nourish your mental, physical, and emotional well-being. For some people, self-care might involve eating more nourishing foods, such as fish, fruit, and vegetables. It might mean cutting out fats and sugar from their diet, or limiting the amount of soda or alcohol they consume. It might also mean trying to change bad habits, such as smoking, or freeing themselves from toxic relationships. It can also involve taking the time to engage in behaviors that reduce stress and are self-soothing, like spending time with friends, taking a bubble bath, exercising, or meditating.

When you take care of yourself physically and emotionally, this is a sign that you respect yourself and feel worthy. It shows that you want to live a healthy and satisfying life and that you are willing to make some sacrifices to do just that. It is for this reason that self-esteem is a major component of self-care, as it is easier to begin a healthy regime when you feel that you are "worth" it. You are more likely to devote the time and energy toward treating yourself with care if you feel that you deserve it to begin with.

In order to ensure that you are engaging in enough self-care, self-awareness is key. Being aware of your negative self-talk and self-defeating attitudes is the first step toward changing them. For example, if you find yourself thinking, "What does it matter if I don't exercise and eat pizza or hamburgers every day?" you can cultivate a healthier attitude, such as, "I am going to start an exercise plan and develop healthier eating habits." When you are aware of your self-defeating thoughts, you can start to change your frame of reference and work toward healthy goals. Instead of feeling sorry for yourself – which can sometimes be easier than actually working to transform unpleasant circumstances – you can try to makes changes that will benefit your well-being. This might entail distancing yourself from unhealthy relationships or changing jobs. It might just involve slightly changing your daily routine or getting a special treat for yourself, such as buying weekly flowers, to add some spice to your life.

Ultimately, finding a purpose or goal – something that gives you a reason to get up in the morning – is extremely important in ensuring that you take care of your emotional and physical needs. It will motive you to work hard, stay focused, and maintain your well-being. This purpose or goal can be whatever you choose it to be. It might include being a good parent, grandparent, friend, or teacher. It might be the desire to be a caregiver, take care of a pet, volunteer your services, or be a writer or artist. It might be to meet with friends or to go to work or school each day. A hobby or special interest might serve as a purpose. Spirituality or faith in a higher power might also serve you well.

The following exercises are intended to help people find the motivation to reduce negativity in their life, engage in pleasurable experiences, get active, and nurture healthier habits. These directives can also help individuals learn the importance of communicating positively with themselves and others, which involves being assertive but also being flexible and finding a lifestyle balance. When individuals regularly engage in self-care and cultivate an awareness of that which does not serve them, they can eventually work to enhance their sense of self-worth and self-acceptance.

Vacation from Anxiety

PROCEDURE: Draw a vacation spot you can visit in order to distance yourself from your stress. The spot may be a realistic place, such as your backyard or a country cabin, or a place in your mind, such as a floating cloud or a magical island. It can be a place you have visited before, such as Chicago or New York, or a place you'd like to visit, such as the Bahamas, Italy, or Spain.

BENEFITS: Engaging in this exercise gives you a chance to breathe, relax, and part with your stress, even for a short while. In this way, you allow yourself to recharge, take inventory of your environment, and allow mindfulness to help you rest and unwind.

QUESTIONS FOR EXPLORATION:

1. What type of place did you draw?

2. Have you visited this place before? Was your visit effective in terms of stress reduction?

3. How can a break from stress be beneficial to your body and mind?

4. When was the last time you chose to release your stress for a while?

5. Do you deserve a retreat from your anxiety?

Chain of Appreciation

ADDITIONAL MATERIALS: Colorful construction paper, scissors, markers, tape or glue, tiny sequins, and glitter.

Procedure: Cut out 30 to 40 strips of colored construction paper that are approximately 6 × 1 inch in size. On each strip, write positive affirmations, upbeat words, and things for which you are grateful. If desired, you can decorate the strips with small designs, images, sequins, and glitter. Next, gently curve one strip into a circle, and tape or glue the ends together. Then, weave a second strip into the first circle to create the next link in the chain. Glue or tape the ends of the second circle together and continue to intertwine each strip together until the chain is complete.

BENEFITS: Creating a chain of appreciation allows you to focus your attention on the "riches" you have in life to help you take care of yourself. This simple project enhances the power of gratitude, which increases life satisfaction and self-esteem. It also promotes an overall sense of well-being because it brings many individuals back to a time when life was simpler, and it was permittable to relax and have uncomplicated fun.

QUESTIONS FOR EXPLORATION:

1. How did you feel while working on the chain? Were you able to give yourself permission to work freely, or did you work in a reluctant manner? If so, what reasons might have caused hesitancy to participate in this exercise?

2. Are you satisfied with the amount of links in your chain? Would you rather it had been longer? Was it easy or difficult to create the chain?

3. Which links are your favorite? Are there any links that gave you pause?

4. Which links would you like to add to this chain in the future?

Personal Road to Recovery

PROCEDURE: Draw your own personal road to recovery. You may add whatever you like to the road that would facilitate your emotional and/or physical well-being. For example, you might include positive self-talk, family, love, support, exercise, assertiveness, hobbies, and making healthy choices. As you draw, think about the quality of the road (e.g., whether it is wide, long, smooth, bumpy, rocky) and where you are located on the road (e.g., beginning, middle, end).

BENEFITS: This exercise allows you to explore your support systems and coping skills, as well as recognize any current obstacles and barriers to wellness.[1] By developing an awareness of the things in your life that you can lean on to enhance your sense of well-being, you are better able to walk the road to recovery.

QUESTIONS FOR EXPLORATION:

1. What type of road did you create? Is it straight, winding, or narrow?

2. Are you alone on the road or are others with you?

3. How do you feel on the road?

4. What else is on the road (e.g., rocks, animals, grass, mud, plants)?

5. Have you been on this road before?

6. Are you ready to walk this road? Are you already walking, or are you running, jumping, skipping, or crawling?

7. Are you taking breaks, or are you pushing yourself to keep going without rest?

8. If you had the ability to change this road, how would you do it?

Self-Soothing Drops

PROCEDURE: Outline a variety of droplet or teardrop shapes, cut them out, and glue them on another sheet of plain white or colorful construction paper. *The group leader may also provide templates of teardrop shapes if participants desire.* Next, fill in the drops with images, words, and phrases that focus on self-comfort. Images might include a smiling face, rainbow, sun, heart, or someone giving themselves a hug. Examples of statements might include: "Just do your best," "This too shall pass," "Take a deep breath," "You are fine as you are," "You can't change others," "Focus on yourself," and "Tomorrow is another day." After you have completed the droplets, you can add a background to your design, such as words, wavy lines, or a rainbow.

BENEFITS: You feel better, less anxious, and increasingly worthy when you choose to self-soothe. The act of taking care of yourself increases your sense of control, self-esteem, and satisfaction with life. You don't feel as stuck, and it puts anger, anxiety, and stress into perspective.

QUESTIONS FOR EXPLORATION:

1. How do the drops represent what you are currently feeling and experiencing?

2. Are there very few drops, a moderate amount, or many drops on the paper?

3. Which drops are most helpful or most significant?

4. How does self-soothing help with stress relief and self-worth?

5. When was the last time you did something to make yourself feel better when you were stressed or felt highly anxious?

Self-Care Toolbox

PROCEDURE: Create an outline of a toolbox and fill it in with a variety of self-care techniques that you can use to cope with difficult situations. List or draw at least five items that you would like to place in your toolbox (e.g., exercise, mediation, yoga, art, journaling, poetry, gardening, baking). Then, decorate the toolbox with designs, shapes, words, and images.

BENEFITS: The more techniques that you have to cope with stress, depression, and anxiety, the stronger and more in control you become. The idea is to pick and choose your coping techniques as needed. Effective techniques will most likely vary according to situation, timing, and your mood, so having a repertoire of skills available in your toolbox will ensure that you are always prepared.

QUESTIONS FOR EXPLORATION:

1. How do the skills you included help you handle stress?

2. Which skills would you like to develop and/or implement in the future?

3. Which techniques have you used in the past that you may need to utilize now?

4. Can you think of a time when a particular coping skill helped you reduce anxiety?

5. Which is your go-to coping skill?

Building Self-Care

PROCEDURE: Draw a large building or another sizeable structure, and fill it in with ways to take care of yourself. For example, the doorway may be filled with bright colors to symbolize positivity, some of the windows may appear to be smiling, a person in a yoga pose may be seen through a large sliding glass door, or a family may be seen through a window eating a healthy meal and laughing with one another. Be as creative as you like.

BENEFITS: Taking care of your needs is important to maintain a healthy sense of self-esteem and to ensure your overall well-being. Practicing self-care allows you to be a better friend and family member, as well as a healthier and more contributing member of society. Your motivation to learn and grow increases as you learn to take healthy risks and not be afraid to make mistakes.

QUESTIONS FOR EXPLORATION:

1. Which part of the building (which self-care method) seems most helpful to you?

2. In relating the building to your own self-care habits, is there room for improvement? What could be changed?

3. How would you characterize the building? Is it impressive and solid, or does it need to be torn down? Is it a place in which you would feel comfortable?

CLIENT RESPONSE:

Betty, a 71-year-old woman experiencing many physical issues and depression, designed this rather pleasant looking house. The door is smiling, and the steps contain affirmations, "One day at a time," and "Breathe." The windows are filled with flowers and people who are smiling, cooking, painting, and dancing. Betty shared that she tries to maintain a positive façade and smiles a lot, but inside she is hurting. She shared that her husband is ill, and she has been trying to deal with arthritis associated with neck and back issues, which incapacitates her at times. Betty accepted compliments and support from group members regarding her sketch but stated that her house needs modernization. She shared that it is falling apart and requires repair, much like herself. She did say she liked that the house is still standing and seemed sturdy.

Behavioral Activation Drawing

PROCEDURE: Behavioral activation is an intervention for depression that involves engaging in meaningful activities that are consistent with the life you want to live. At the core of behavioral activation is activity scheduling, which involves creating a daily schedule of activities that bring you a sense of pleasure and mastery, that are consistent with your values, and that decrease avoidance and isolation. To create your own behavioral activation drawing, take a piece of paper and fill the page with shapes, images, magazine photos, words, and phrases that symbolize the ways in which you want to get active. This can include work or professional goals, hobbies, interests, and other positive activities to help create a life that is uplifting and productive.

BENEFITS: When individuals are depressed or anxious, they tend to isolate and engage in avoidance behaviors, which only serves to exacerbate their symptoms. By engaging in behavioral activation, people can learn to get more active and start engaging in behaviors that nourish their physical and emotional health. Similarly, creating a behavioral activation drawing can help you become more aware of productive and purposeful ways to structure and spend your free time. You can then begin to put leisure and work-related goals into practice.

QUESTIONS FOR EXPLORATION:

1. Which images seem most meaningful right now?

2. Are your hobbies and interests depicted in your artwork?

3. What, if any, barriers have been developed over the years that stop you from pursuing goals and engaging in enriching activities?

4. What does your daily schedule currently look like? Is it satisfying? If not, how can it be improved?

Focus on Motivation

PROCEDURE: Write an affirmation, positive phrase, or uplifting word in the center of the paper and sketch images and designs related to the phrase in the background. For example, if you chose the affirmation, "Go with the flow," then you might draw images of a stream with flowing water or someone surfing on a pattern of wavy, pastel-like colors. Similarly, if you chose the affirmation, "I am strong," then you might draw images of body builders, mountains, or trees with thick trunks and a multitude of branches.

BENEFITS: Through the use of motivating words and phrases, this exercise helps increase self-worth by inspiring you to pursue your dreams and goals.

QUESTIONS FOR EXPLORATION:

1. How does the affirmation chosen as the focal point of your design inspire you?

2. What is the primary message of your artwork?

3. Who or what tends to help encourage or motivate you to follow your dreams and pursue your objectives?

4. In which ways do affirmations increase self-esteem and positive thinking?

Motivating Intention Stick

ADDITIONAL MATERIALS: Sticks or twigs; yarn, string, twine, or ribbon.

PROCEDURE: The following directive is adapted from Jennifer Kind-Rubin.[2] Begin this exercise by going for a walk outside, somewhere that is quiet and peaceful. As you walk, feel your feet connect to the earth as they hit the ground. Notice what your skin feels like as it basks in the warmth of the sun. Breathe in the air, and listen to the soundtrack of the natural environment. As you mindfully take in this moment, pause for a moment, close your eyes, and set an intention yourself. This can be an intention for your day, your week, or your month. What word or words come to mind? How do you want to show up to the world? Slowly open your eyes and begin walking with intention. As you return home, collect some branches or twigs to use for your artwork.

Return to your intention, and write or paint your intention onto the branch. You may also paint the branch first before writing on it. Then, take a piece of yarn, string, twine, or ribbon and begin to wrap it around the branch. With each wrapping movement, you are securing your intention in place. You can use a variety of colors and textures to make it unique to you. When you are done wrapping the branch, decorate it however you desire using paint, glitter, sequins, or other materials. Finally, place your intention where you can regularly see it so it serves as a visual reminder of what you hope to accomplish or create.

BENEFITS: Creating intention sticks help you become mindful, aware, and attentive to possible goals and ways you want to live your life. The stick serves as a tangible item you can refer to for inspiration, clarity and motivation . As you design it you are ideally thinking about your priorities, plans and ways to achieve them. Designing the stick provides the opportunity to create colors and patterns that relate to your mood and hope for following a certain life path. For example, a bright red stick with glitter may relate to excitement or change and a rustic, simple stick may relate to a life of simplicity and authenticity.

QUESTIONS FOR EXPLORATION:

1. What messages are conveyed through the design of your intention stick?

2. What are some of your immediate and future goals?

3. In addition to this intention stick, how can you motivate yourself to follow your dreams and objectives?

Simplifying This Exercise: *The group leader will have already gathered sticks and will provide them for clients after the guided imagery exercise. Group members will engage in a brief guided imagery where they close their eyes for a few minutes and imagine they are walking through a lush wooded area, observing the beautiful scenery, feeling calm and peaceful while looking mindfully for sticks to use for this intention exercise. Ask participants to imagine they are choosing, gathering, and then mindfully holding the sticks as they calmly walk back to the facility. Next, provide the sticks for clients, allowing them to choose the ones that appeal to them. Then, continue with the rest of the steps included in the directions to complete this project.*

CLIENT RESPONSE:

Diane, a 48-year-old woman recovering from a major depressive episode, began designing this intention stick by writing a few important reminders on various parts of it using a permanent black marker. She wrote *"Accept change,"* *"Be more ambitious,"* *"Want but not need others,"* and *"Add color to my life, not be so gray."* Next Diane began wrapping yarn, ribbon and string around the stick, gently covering those very important thoughts, using both glue and tape to adhere the strands. Lastly, she added colorful sequins and a small stone to represent the addition of color to her life, and to symbolize change and hope for a happier new year.

She shared that creating the stick was significant because it helped her focus and symbolize her intentions into something that she could see and touch. Diane remarked she was excited to bring her project home and show it to her husband who always wondered what she did in creative therapy groups. She added that her husband might better understand her current state of mind when she explains the way she designed the stick and its significance.

Straw Attribute Mandala

ADDITIONAL MATERIALS: About 100 paper or plastic straws.

PROCEDURE: Using a paper plate, make an outline of a circle on a large piece of paper to form a mandala. Then, glue straws on the perimeter of the circle about an inch or so apart, so that they are emanating out from the circle like sunrays. Next, cut pieces of paper into small, narrow rectangles and write positive qualities about yourself on each rectangle, such as, "I am a devoted friend," or "I am honest and trustworthy." Finally, glue the attributes on the straws in varying places (top, bottom, or middle). Decorate the rest of the mandala using markers, pastels, etc.

BENEFITS: This exercise promotes increased self-awareness and inspiration, increased feelings of positivity and possibilities, and reduction of fears and doubts about one's abilities. Self-esteem and positivity are enhanced as you choose, write, acknowledge, and then glue affirming words, traits and characteristics to this unique, personalized mandala.

QUESTIONS FOR EXPLORATION:

1. Which attributes can you accept today?

2. Which ones are you most proud of and willing to share?

3. How does your mandala represent your personality and attitude toward yourself and others?

240

My Protective Fence

PROCEDURE: Draw a fence that protects you from fears, intruders, anxiety, and worries.

BENEFITS: A fence can serve you both positively and negatively. It can protect you from harm, but it can also create a wall between you and the outside world. It can stop you from taking healthy risks and moving forward. By illustrating your own protective fence, you develop self-awareness of any barriers, obstacles, or avoidance behaviors getting in the way of your physical and emotional well-being.

QUESTIONS FOR EXPLORATION:

1. How large and strong is your fence?

2. What is its purpose?

3. Is it helpful or harmful? Why?

4. What or whom does it allow inside?

5. How long has it been in place?

6. Do you want to make changes to it? What might you change about it?

Escaping from Fear

PROCEDURE: Draw yourself or a fictitious figure escaping from a frightening, threatening, or uncomfortable situation.

BENEFITS: This exercise helps you examine how you see yourself in relation to your environment. For example, do you see yourself as strong or meek? Large or small? Able to accept challenges or unable to rise to the occasion? By developing this awareness, you can better assess how you react to challenges and upsetting life events. Reflecting on your thoughts and reactions to this exercise can increase insight and help you develop a plan of action to utilize when you are feeling afraid and anxious.

QUESTIONS FOR EXPLORATION:

1. What is the figure escaping from and how is it escaping?

2. Does the escape route appear effective?

3. How does the figure seem to react in the situation? Would you react in a similar manner?

4. Is the figure feeling fearful, terrified, courageous, panicky, or something else?

5. Will the figure escape unscathed, or will there be repercussions from this event?

Coping with the Holidays

PROCEDURE: On one side of the page, draw your feelings about the holidays. You can focus on whatever holiday is approaching and might be of concern. On the other side of the paper, draw coping techniques you can use to deal with any negative emotions that this holiday might elicit. For example, you can draw an artist's palette to represent a focus on art for stress reduction, a figure in a yoga position to symbolize mindfulness, a pet to signify unconditional love, or smiling faces to represent the importance of practicing gratitude to lift your spirits. You can include realistic or abstract images, as well as words, in your drawing.

BENEFITS: This exercise helps you cope with ambivalent or stressful feelings that you may have about the holidays by reminding you to focus on the positive and by encouraging you to explore self-care practices you can use to manage the anxiety, stress, loneliness, or frustration that is often associated with the holidays.

QUESTIONS FOR EXPLORATION:

1. How would you describe your thoughts and feelings regarding the holiday?

2. Will this holiday be different from previous ones?

3. Will you "choose" to focus on the negative or positive aspects of the day?

4. What are your coping mechanisms?

5. What is one special thing you can do for yourself on this day? How can you show yourself compassion?

Sprouting Self-Worth

PROCEDURE: Draw a shape, figure, pet, plant, animal (real or imaginary), or a profile of a person sprouting *your* positive attributes. Some of these attributes may include kindness, honesty, compassion, having a good sense of humor, or being a good cook.

BENEFITS: This exercise enhances self-esteem, self-awareness, and motivation. It reminds us to celebrate and nurture ourselves, much as we nurture our plants, pets, and close friends and family.

QUESTIONS FOR EXPLORATION:

1. What is sprouting from the focal point of the picture?

2. Which positive traits make you feel most proud?

3. In reference to "sprouting," are your positive characteristics newly planted seeds, seeds that are now beginning to bud, buds about to bloom, or flowers that are blooming?

4. How can you nurture your healthy traits?

5. What do you need to avoid in order to keep your blooms growing?

Personal Health Charger

PROCEDURE: Draw your own unique "charger" (something that helps you regain motivation and vigor) and add ways in which you can recharge. For example, this may involve getting enough sleep, taking cat naps, eating a balanced diet, or thinking in a positive manner. Feel free to be playful in your response.

BENEFITS: By illustrating your own personal charger, you can explore ways in which you can engage in self-care techniques that facilitate emotional and physical renewal. In particular, you can examine ways to increase your energy and motivation.

QUESTIONS FOR EXPLORATION:

1. What is unique about your charger?

2. What does it look like?

3. How does it work and how effective is it?

4. Do you currently need extra help to feel energetic?

5. What techniques do you use to recharge now and what ideas do you have about recharging in the future?

CLIENT RESPONSE:

Pat, an 18-year-old woman experiencing depression and anxiety, drew her golden retriever, Mel. Pat shared that Mel is loving, sweet, and playful, and snuggles with her when she feels sad. She remarked that she has no choice but to be energized when she is with Mel because Mel loves active play, especially with his blue ball, which is a focal point of the sketch. Pat stated that Mel will bring her the ball and wait enthusiastically for her to throw it across the yard so he can run after it, fetch it, and play this favorite game over and over again. Pat shared that she often feels better, even if only temporarily, when she is with Mel, whom she calls her best friend.

Black Cloud Overhead

PROCEDURE: Sketch a self-representative figure and draw a black cloud (representing depression, anger, worry, or stress) over the figure (or somewhere in the vicinity of it).

BENEFITS: Engaging in this directive aids in the exploration of negativity, anxiety, and sadness, and it helps you recognize the ways in which these emotions affect various aspects of your life. By developing an awareness of these destructive attitudes, you can better examine coping mechanisms (e.g., acceptance, distraction, mindfulness) to help you make healthier choices that get you through difficult moments.

QUESTIONS FOR EXPLORATION:

1. How large is the cloud? Does it appear threatening or nondescript?

2. What does the relationship look like between the figure and the cloud? For instance, are they about equal in size and weight, or does one of them overwhelm the other?

3. Is the cloud directly overhead or to the side of the figure? What would either position signify in terms of your mood, attitude, outlook, and behavior?

4. Is the cloud always there, or are there days when the sun is out?

5. Are there benefits to having the cloud around?

6. What are the consequences of the cloud?

7. If the cloud is an unwanted guest, how can you support its departure?

8. How can you deal with it and still function in the event that the cloud is stubborn and won't move right now?

9. Using an umbrella as a metaphor, how can you protect yourself from the possible rain (e.g., problems, unhappiness) that the cloud may bring?

CLIENT RESPONSE:

Hailey, a 30-year-old woman with bipolar disorder, drew herself being "sucked in" by the dark cloud. Hailey shared that she felt out of control in all areas of her life. She stated that her moods were very changeable and drastically hurt her relationship with her boyfriend. She complained that she was also ruining her chances for a better job and true friendships, which she desperately wanted to develop with coworkers.

She remarked that she needed to find ways to control herself, especially her anger, which was often incongruent with the reason for her fury. She would blow up over little things, such as her boyfriend buying the wrong sandwich bread or leaving one dish in the sink. Hailey mentioned that she knew she needed to take her medication as prescribed instead of stopping it when she began to feel better. She said she self-medicated because she hated feeling dull and tired when she took her mood stabilizers.

Throwing Out Problems and Negativity

PROCEDURE: Draw a garbage can in the center of the page, and fill it with images, words, and symbols representing all the people, places, thoughts, feelings, relationships, and items you want to throw out, gain control over, or stop dwelling upon constantly.

BENEFITS: Symbolically throwing out negativity is the first step toward being free. It gives you some measure of control and provides you with perspective regarding what you need to keep and what is garbage. It may be time to declutter your home, mind, and lifestyle.

QUESTIONS FOR EXPLORATION:

1. What is in your garbage can?

2. How full is it?

3. What is your reaction to the items it contains? Were you surprised to see some of the items in it?

4. What are some of the steps you can take in reality to rid yourself of anxiety, negativity or toxic relationships?

5. Is there any garbage that you are not ready to throw away just yet?

6. What lessons have you learned from the contents of your garbage can?

CLIENT RESPONSE:

Daniel, a 32-year-old man with bipolar disorder, added a variety of "junk" to his garbage can. The bottom layer is filled with his favorite colors (shades of blue) representing his depression. Daniel remarked that he is not able to appreciate anything he liked in the past – not even his favorite colors – and, therefore, he wanted to throw his despair away in order to feel "normal" again. He also added a fiery, red rage that "combines with my anxiety." Dollar signs represent financial problems, and a black figure situated within the can symbolizes his wife of two years who has become, as per Daniel, "a real problem." His boss is hanging, "but not being hung," outside the garbage can to represent Daniel's need to change jobs and think about going back to college so he could pursue his dream of becoming a veterinarian.

Assertiveness and Boundaries

PROCEDURE: Draw a self-representative figure with its hand held up, as if the figure is trying to demonstrate its specific boundaries to keep someone away. Next, surround the figure with sketches, images, and words representing which of *your* boundaries need to be respected.

BENEFITS: Focusing on assertiveness helps you feel in greater control, and it also increases your ability to take care of your emotional and physical well-being. Your boundaries define your space and allow you the freedom to be yourself and function in a safe and effective manner.

QUESTIONS FOR EXPLORATION:

1. What message is your figure communicating? Are you pleased with its message?

2. Are you able to assert yourself when needed?

3. What may stop you from getting your needs met?

4. When was the last time you were able to say "no" to a request, demand, or infiltration of your boundaries?

5. How does maintaining boundaries and assertiveness promote better self-care?

6. How would your life change if you acted in a more assertive manner?

Your Backpack

PROCEDURE: Create a drawing of your backpack, which is a symbol of the problems, stress, worry, and resentments you are holding on to or carrying every day. As you draw, think about the size and weight of your backpack. You may also represent your backpack with a realistic image or any item, design, or shape you desire.

BENEFITS: This exercise allows you to explore any negativity that you may be holding on to that is wearing you down and stopping you from achieving goals, greater happiness, healthy motivation, or better relationships and peace. Increasing self-awareness of this negativity will allow you to better develop coping techniques to lessen resentment, anger, and unpleasant thoughts.

QUESTIONS FOR EXPLORATION:

1. How did you represent your backpack, and how much weight are you carrying?

2. How is the weight affecting you emotionally and physically?

3. Is there anything you can take out of your backpack to make your load lighter?

4. Is holding on to the weight helping you or hurting you?

5. How long have you had your backpack? How long has it weighed what it weighs now?

6. What would your ideal backpack look like and feel like on your back?

Ice Packs for Healing

PROCEDURE: Draw two or more unique, personal ice packs that will help reduce swelling (e.g., stress and discomfort) and help you heal from physical or emotional pain. What are your ice packs filled with that promote your well-being (e.g., love, support, chicken soup, a good night's sleep, your pet)?

BENEFITS: Drawing your own ice packs for healing reminds you of your responsibility to take an active role in your own healing and well-being. It encourages you to look for ways in which you can engage in self-care and practice self-compassion.

QUESTIONS FOR EXPLORATION:

1. What do your ice packs look like? Are they large or small? Are they soft, hard, colorful, freezing cold, or just cold enough to hold? Are they easy or difficult to hold and manipulate?

2. In which ways do they help you?

3. Do you need to use the ice packs now? Have you needed them in the past?

4. How does it feel when you place them on your skin or wherever they need to be?

5. Do you keep them at home for emergencies or are they difficult to find?

6. Have you ever left them on so long that you received a burn? How did that feel? How long did it take the burn to heal?

7. Who tends to administer them?

CLIENT RESPONSE:

A 68-year-old woman named Fay drew two purple and pink, heart-shaped ice packs, sharing that they are much needed to soothe her frequent incapacitating migraine headaches. She stated that the ice packs are very soft and filled with lavender and love. Fay mentioned that she is always looking for new ways to self-soothe.

Currently, she rests in a darkened room and attempts to sleep to escape the discomfort and associated nausea of her headaches. Fay remarked that her headaches are sometimes brought on by stress and anxiety related to her fear of being alone. She said she often feels lonely, believing that if she had more love in her life, her headaches would lessen. She knew that a major goal was to volunteer and join social groups to meet new people

Boundaries within Relationships

PROCEDURE: Draw or find magazine photos that represent your boundaries in the context of interpersonal relationships (e.g., the ways you distance yourself from people when they try to invade your physical and emotional space).

BENEFITS: Boundaries reflect your right to independence, safety, and freedom. By defining and holding fast to your boundaries, you can maintain your sense of individual identity. You give yourself permission to choose your beliefs, friends, and partners, as well as to express your feelings, emotions, and concerns. You are able to better take care of yourself, and your relationships become healthier and happier.

QUESTIONS FOR EXPLORATION:

1. Which boundaries are set in your artwork?

2. Are the boundaries clear and distinct or hazy?

3. How difficult is it for you to set boundaries in your relationships? Are you able to deny requests that are stressful or unappealing?

4. Are you able to separate yourself (e.g., your feelings, emotions, etc.) from others?

5. What types of limits are you currently setting or in the process of setting within your relationships?

6. How would setting boundaries in relationships help you to better take care of yourself?

CLIENT RESPONSE:

Ron, a 40-year-old man with addiction issues, wrote "Carpe Diem" on the page in large letters to symbolize the way he attempts to maintain emotional boundaries. Ron shared that negative thoughts are always popping into his head, so he has to be mindful and think positively to counteract them. He added a sun to remember to be optimistic, but above the sun are layers of clouds, and he is standing in rows of fire. Ron stated that the fire often tries to overtake him, and it is a struggle to "not get burned." He also shared that he attempts to maintain emotional boundaries by focusing on one problem at a time, going to Narcotics Anonymous and Alcoholics Anonymous, taking it day by day, and reciting the serenity prayer a few times a day. He also remarked that his wife helps by reminding him to stay calm and in the moment.

Healing from Head to Toe

PROCEDURE: Draw a self-representative outline of a person that covers most of the page. *The group leader can also distribute an outline of the human form to those who desire more structure.* Beginning at the figure's feet and working your way up, use colors, shapes, words, and images to label or sketch ways you can heal each part of the body. Suggested body parts include your feet, legs, stomach, arms, hands, back, shoulder, neck, lips, eyes, or head. You may also include organs, such as the heart and the brain, when considering how to heal.

BENEFITS: This exercise promotes self-awareness and self-care by allowing you to symbolically heal your mind and body in a focused, artistic, and mindful manner. When generalized to actual care, this symbolic act of caring may lead to improved psychological and physical health, as well as improved energy, motivation, and self-esteem.

QUESTIONS FOR EXPLORATION:

1. How would you describe the figure you created?

2. Where is healing needed the most?

3. What steps can you take to begin or continue the healing process?

4. Which methods have proven most effective so far in your recovery?

5. Which part of your body seems to be the strongest?

6. What do you do on a daily basis that helps you function as well as possible?

Psychological Safety Net

PROCEDURE: Draw a picture of what your safety net looks like, which is representative of the things in your life that keep you from falling or from experiencing psychological or emotional harm.

BENEFITS: Just as tightrope walkers use a safety net in case they lose their balance and fall, it is also advantageous for you to have a safety net in case you relapse, have a setback, feel frightened, are unsure, or need extra help and support.

QUESTIONS FOR EXPLORATION:

1. What type of safety net did you draw?

2. How strong is your net? Can you depend on it?

3. Have you ever used your safety net?

4. Do you know anyone else who might benefit from a safety net?

CLIENT RESPONSE:

Jeff, a 29-year-old man with bipolar disorder and addiction issues, drew his safety net as an old-fashioned movie screen and projector. He shared that he occasionally works as an extra for movies and television shows and finds the work exciting and enjoyable. Jeff remarked that he loves dressing up as characters from different periods in history, especially the early 1900s, and he enjoys the camaraderie of his fellow actors. He remarked that the work keeps him focused and allows him "to step outside of himself" for a while.

Taking Yourself on a Date

PROCEDURE: *The group leader should begin the session by asking participants, "How do you treat yourselves?" and "Who will go above and beyond to treat themselves well?"* Consider how you currently treat yourself and whether you currently provide yourself with enough self-care. Examples of self-care include: buying luxuries for yourself, like roses; finding time in the middle of the day for a bubble bath; reading a good book; or cooking yourself a healthy, delicious meal. Then, create a piece of art with the theme "Taking yourself on a date" to consider how you can provide yourself with self-care. Think about what you would do, where you would go, how you might feel, and the mood you would ideally create on the date (e.g., calm, peaceful, romantic).

BENEFITS: This exercise helps you explore the extent to which you are kind to yourself or whether you need to work more diligently on self-care. By considering how you would take yourself out on a date, you are able to examine the significance of treating yourself as well or better than you treat others because "you are worth it." Similar to traveling on an airplane, you need to provide yourself with oxygen first before you can be of service to others.

QUESTIONS FOR EXPLORATION:

1. How was the date represented?

2. What would make you happiest on a date?

3. Do you feel entitled to be treated well?

4. What is the first step you could take to self-soothe and be kind to yourself?

5. What is the best date you ever went on with someone else or by yourself? What made it so special?

CLIENT RESPONSE:

Ellen, a 41-year-old woman with depression, shared that she would take herself to the seashore. She remarked that she would lay in the sun while listening to her favorite radio station and let the sun's warm rays sweep over her. She would take a quick dip in the ocean and then take herself out for a lovely seafood dinner. Ellen sighed after sharing this imaginary date, stating that in reality she would never take herself on a date because she was afraid to be by herself in public. She said she had great difficulty even going to the supermarket by herself; she felt so self-conscious. Ellen remarked that she was trying to be more independent and taking tiny steps every day toward accomplishing this very difficult goal.

notes & credits

CHAPTER 1

1. Christopher K. Germer and Kristin D. Neff, "Self-Compassion in Clinical Practice," *Journal of Clinical Psychology: In Session* 69, no. 8 (2013): 856–867.
2. "Self-friendly" as used in this context means self-compassionate; it is not in the standard dictionary.
3. This project may be presented in a variety of ways depending on the clientele you are working with at the time. If you are working with trauma survivors, then make sure to know the participants well, and gear the project toward their needs and current psychological state.
4. Permanent markers work well for mask design. When you have a longer period of time to engage in this project, add collage materials, such as cut paper, magazine photos, foam pieces, small stones, glitter, and paint.
5. Susan I. Buchalter, *Stick Figure Affirmations: Cartoons to Lift the Spirit* (USA: Amazon Publication, 2018).
6. This exercise is based on an idea by Evelyn Sutkowski, LPC, LCADC.
7. ModPodge is a thin glue that can be purchased at most art supply stores, including S&S and Nasco art supplies.
8. This project was presented as a result of a dream shared by a client.

CHAPTER 2

1. Jon Kabat-Zinn, *Mindfulness for Beginners* (Boulder, CO: Sounds True, 2006).
2. "Acceptance and Commitment Therapy," Getselfhelp.co.uk, accessed June 17, 2019, http://getselfhelp.co.uk/act.htm.
3. "What is Mindfulness?" Mindfulness: Finding Peace in a Frantic World, accessed June 17, 2019, http://franticworld.com/what-is-mindfulness/.
4. Christopher Germer, "What is Mindfulness?" *Insight Journal* 22 (2004): 24–29.
5. *Encyclopedia.com*, s.v. "Sacred Space," accessed June 17, 2019, https://www.encyclopedia.com/environment/encyclopedias-almanacs-transcripts-and-maps/sacred-space.
6. This is a slightly modified version of a mindfulness exercise that was led by Essie Larson, Ph.D., on November 14, 2018, at the Penn Medicine Princeton House Behavioral Health Workshop.
7. The Trixie Doodle was developed by this author and is used with clients to unwind, laugh, and reduce anxiety.
8. This art directive is modified from the "Drawing Your Breath" exercise presented by Carolyn Mehlomakulu, LMFT-S, ATR-BC, at http://creativityintherapy.com/2017/08/drawing-your-breath-a-mindful-art-exercise/.
9. *The Free Dictionary*, s.v. "Mantra," accessed June 17, 2019, https://www.thefreedictionary.com/mantra.

10. "What is a Mantra?" EOC Institute, accessed June 17, 2019, https://eocinstitute.org/meditation/how-mantras-enhance-meditation/.

11. "What is a Mantra?" EOC Institute.

12. "What is Spirituality?" Taking Charge of Your Health and Wellbeing, University of Minnesota, accessed June 17, 2019, https://www.takingcharge.csh.umn.edu/what-spirituality.

13. *Vocabulary.com*, s.v. "Intuitive," accessed June 17, 2019, https://www.vocabulary.com/dictionary/intuitive.

14. Giora Carmi, "Intuitive Flow Through Artwork," *Psychology Tomorrow* (blog), August 3, 2014, http://psychologytomorrowmagazine.com/intuitive-flow-artwork/.

CHAPTER 3

1. A photo of a fist may be presented to assist participants who want to design a realistic fist. Of course, they can also copy their own fist.

2. Project description and benefits are modified from the work of Meg Krugel, which is available at https://thesoupladle.wordpress.com/.

3. This directive was brought to fruition following a brief discussion regarding coping techniques with Judith Mecklenburger, LCSW.

4. Alternatively, clients may sculpt their stress stone from clay. During discussion, they may choose to keep their stone or throw it in a garbage can placed in the center of the room to represent ridding themselves from their stress.

5. Depending on the length of the session, larger sheets may be distributed, and the outlines would ideally increase in size. In this way, participants would have more time to include detail and work on a larger scale. The small scale suggested in this exercise works well for a brief intervention.

6. Deah Schwartz, "Expressive Arts Therapy Idea: Mapping Out Change," *Art Therapy* (blog), accessed June 17, 2019, http://www.arttherapyblog.com/art-therapy-ideas/mapping-out-change/#.XAWdiGeWypo.

7. For this directive, the term "doppelgänger" refers to an evil twin who is out of control. This exercise was suggested by a 29-year-old client who thought of the activity while playing video games at home. Group members were very pleased with the name "doppelgänger," and they were both amused and motivated to work on the project.

8. Marsha Linehan, *Cognitive-Behavioral Treatment of Borderline Personality Disorder* (New York, NY: Guildford Press, 1993).

CHAPTER 4

1. *Vocabulary.com*, s.v. "Happiness," accessed June 17, 2019, https://www.vocabulary.com/dictionary/happiness.

2. Sonja Lyubomirsky, *The How of Happiness* (New York, NY: Penguin Press, 2007).

3. Tara Parker-Pope, "How to Be Happy," *The New York Times*, November 15, 2017, https://www.nytimes.com/guides/well/how-to-be-happy.

4. If it is difficult to draw the tree, then copy and paste a tree from Google Images, or design an abstract tree.

5. "What is a Rube Goldberg Machine?" Wonderopolis, National Center for Families Learning, accessed June 17, 2019, https://wonderopolis.org/wonder/what-is-a-rube-goldberg-machine.

6. This quote was shared by an art therapy client.

7. Cynthia M. Thaik, "Gratitude: Soul Food," *Psychology Today*, May 7, 2013, https://www.psychologytoday.com/us/blog/the-heart/201305/gratitude-soul-food.

8. Jennifer Evans, "Earth Laughs in Flowers – Ralph Waldo Emerson," *Immerse* (blog), Center for Positive Organizations, November 3, 2015, https://positiveorgs.bus.umich.edu/blog/earth-laughs-in-flowers-ralph-waldo-emerson/.

CHAPTER 5

1. Rotten Tomatoes and the Tomatometer score are the world's most trusted recommendation resources for quality entertainment. The Tomatometer score represents the percentage of professional critic reviews that are positive for a given film or television show.

2. This phrase was stated by an art therapy client in 2019.

CHAPTER 6

1. "What is Self-Esteem?" Owning It Therapy & Counseling Services, accessed June 17, 2019, http://www.owning-it.com/self-esteem-anxiety/self-esteem/.

2. "Our Urgent Need for Self-Esteem," NathanielBranden.com, Nathaniel Branden, accessed June 17, 2019, http://www.nathanielbranden.com/our-urgent-need-for-self-esteem.

3. Leon F. Seltzer, "The Path to Unconditional Self-Acceptance," *Psychology Today*, September 10, 2008, https://www.psychologytoday.com/us/blog/evolution-the-self/200809/the-path-unconditional-self-acceptance.

4. Zorka Hereford, "Examples of Positive Affirmations," Essential Life Skills, accessed June 17, 2019, https://www.essentiallifeskills.net/positiveaffirmations.html.

CHAPTER 7

1. This exercise is helpful for emotional recovery, as well as recovery from addictions.

2. Jennifer Kind-Rubin, "Intention Sticks," JKR Psychotherapy, March 17, 2015, http://jkrtherapy.com/new-blog-1/2015/3/17/intention-sticks.